THE CRITICS RAVE!

Like I said to my son, Irving the doctor (a regular prince), this book is a real mechayeh.[1] It made me forget my aggravation for the first time in thirty-seven years. It worked better than prune juice and Ex-lax, already. It made me forget that my sons didn't finish their chicken soup this morning, that my daughter Milly is going with a poor goy, and that I'm only going to get an eighty-five percent discount on my new mink stole.

I'm going to share this book with all of the girls in my Mah-Jongg game at Grossinger's (because they don't have money to spend on books—unless they have a relative who can get them a good deal).

But the rest of you . . . buy it! Give a copy to your bubba.[2] It will make her smile. It will even take her mind off the payments on the Miami condominium. Altogether, it's more laughs than fiddling on your roof or having a nagila!

—Goldie Berkowitz, Literary Editor
The Yenta Lunchtime Dispatch

[1] a tr
[2] gran

Also by Larry Wilde

THE OFFICIAL POLISH/ITALIAN JOKE BOOK

THE OFFICIAL
JEWISH/IRISH
JOKE BOOK

by
Larry Wilde

Illustrations by Ron Wing

PINNACLE BOOKS • NEW YORK CITY

THE OFFICIAL JEWISH/IRISH JOKE BOOK

Text copyright © 1974 by Larry Wilde
Illustrations copyright © 1974 by Pinnacle Books, Inc.

An original Pinnacle Books edition, published for the first time anywhere.

ISBN: 0-523-00320-X

First printing, June 1974
Second printing, September 1975
Third printing, February 1976
Fourth printing, February 1977

Printed in the United States of America

PINNACLE BOOKS, INC.
275 Madison Avenue
New York, N.Y. 10016

This book is dedicated to Milton Josefsberg,
my friend, my golf partner, and my tutor,
with grateful appreciation.
and
To Gertie and Selig,
who made it all possible.

ABOUT THE AUTHOR

When Larry Wilde was asked about his ethnic qualifications for authoring this book, he replied, "I'm Jewish, and I grew up in an Irish neighborhood!"

Mr. Wilde is also a popular nightclub and television comedian who has performed at the major entertainment spots with Debbie Reynolds, Ann-Margret, Sonny and Cher, Wayne Newton, Vikki Carr, and Pat Boone. In addition, Larry is frequently seen on TV in commercials, on talk shows, and on such series as "Adam 12," "Barnaby Jones," and "The Mary Tyler Moore Show."

Born in Jersey City, New Jersey, Mr. Wilde received a bachelor's degree from the University of Miami, Florida. His writing credits include articles for professional journals as well as for *Penthouse*, *TV Guide*, *Genesis*, *Coronet*, and other popular magazines.

Larry Wilde is also the author of the best-selling *The Official Polish/Italian Joke Book* and *The Great Comedians* (Citadel Press).

THE OFFICIAL
JEWISH
JOKE BOOK

INTRODUCTION   1

1. SHALOM   5
   Israel ... Egypt ... Arabs ... Tourists

2. SHMALTZ   21
   Chicken Fat ... Catskills ... Cooking
   Mink ... Married Life ... Relatives

3. SHTICK   39
   Glossary of Jewish Terms

4. SHMATTES   41
   Clothing Business ... Sons-in-law ...
   Money Partners ... Prostitutes

5. SHMOOZE   61
   Chattering ... Children ... Miami
   Beach ... Grandmothers ... Sex

6. SHTOOPS   83
   Jewish Curses

7. SHOCHETS   87
   Doctors ... Dentists ... Medicine

8. SHABBAS   99
   Sabbath ... Synagogue ... Religion ...
   Rabbis ... Priests

INTRODUCTION

Does your heart ache? Laugh it off!
—Jewish Folk Saying

Comedy experts have long discussed, theorized, and analyzed the "Jewish sense of humor." Some say it has been a guiding light through the dark centuries of prejudice and pogroms.

It seems as though no other people in the history of mankind have contributed more generously to the advancement of the jest. Much of the laughter in today's entertainment media is provided by Jewish comedy writers and comedians. These dedicated jokesmiths create the merriment that helps make living just a little cheerier. Witness this bit of persiflage directed toward a

1

member of the cloth—as told by the veteran television writer, Milt Josefsberg:

Some years ago, Rabbi Aaron Wise of our Valley Jewish Community Center, took ill. While he was recuperating, we sent him this telegram:

DEAR RABBI: YOU WILL BE HAPPY TO KNOW THAT THE TEMPLE BOARD OF DIRECTORS WISH YOU A SPEEDY RECOVERY BY A VOTE OF 12 TO 7.

Jews have a heritage of joke-making. It has been the pin with which they have pricked the thick-walled bubble of adversity. It has also been their chief means of expressing the gaiety and exuberant lust for life that is so typically Jewish.

The "chosen people" have taught themselves to laugh. Better yet, they have learned to laugh at themselves. The following story, circulated during the Nazi reign of terror in World War II, best illustrates the Jewish comedic point of view:

Berger, hiding with his wife from the Nazis in a secluded Berlin attic, decided to get a breath of fresh air. While out walking he came face to face with Adolf Hitler.

The German leader pulled out a gun and pointed to a pile of horse manure in the street. "All right, Jew!" he shouted, "eat that or I'll kill you!" Trembling, Berger did as he was ordered.

Hitler began laughing so hard he dropped the weapon. Berger picked it up and said, "Now, you eat the manure or I'll shoot!" The Führer got down on his hands and knees and began eating.

While he was occupied, Berger sneaked away, ran through an alley, climbed over a fence, and dashed up the stairs to the attic. He slammed the door shut, bolted and locked it securely. "Hilda! Hilda!" he exclaimed to his wife. "Guess who I had lunch with today!"

Jewish jokes can be acidly satiric, but for the most part they are full of gentle tolerance for human frailty. Many are tongue-in-cheek slaps at avarice, hypocrisy, and smug stupidity, but, almost always, they are the fun-loving means to laugh off a heartache.

The quips, gags, and stories in this collection typify the "Jewish sense of humor." As Harry Golden, the well-known wit, raconteur, and author put it: "Enjoy! Enjoy!"

LARRY WILDE
Hollywood, California

June, 1974

SHALOM

Out of the Middle East conflicts have come much heartbreak and tragedy—and comedy. Despite the bloodshed and bitter desert warfare, Israel managed a smile. Here are some of the classic lines that turned tears to laughter:

After fighting only twenty-four hours, the Israelis released the following communiqué:
TODAY WE DOWNED 900 PLANES. 600 DEFINITE. 300 PLEDGED.

* * *

ISRAELI ENLISTMENT POSTER
Join the Army and See the Pyramids

* * *

An Israeli soldier apologized for capturing only 8 tanks and 250 prisoners. "After all, my husband wasn't with me!"

5

Two foot soldiers in Jerusalem were talking over a glass of tea.

"What's our goal today?"

"We capture the Suez Canal!"

"Good! But what'll we do in the afternoon?"

* * *

How do you know an Egyptian flag when you see it?

It's all white!

* * *

WORLD'S THINNEST BOOK
Arab Military Victories

* * *

Israeli Intelligence has discovered a key Egyptian military photo. It's a picture of the Arabs practicing war maneuvers—throwing their hands up in the air.

* * *

At one point in the campaign, an Arab division spotted a lone Israeli sniper on a sand dune. The commander dispatched three men to get him. When they didn't return, he sent a dozen. None of them came back. Finally he sent an entire company.

Two hours later, one blood-splattered Egyptian soldier crawled back. "It was an ambush," he muttered. "There were *two* of them!"

* * *

"I th-th-think the Israelis sh-sh-should g-g-give b-b-back all the Arab t-t-territory and g-g-get the hell out of E-g-g-gypt!"

"Sure, that's easy for you to say!"

* * *

Egyptian President Sadat made a brief appearance on the Cairo television show "Where's My Line?"

* * *

Ralph Nader has launched a campaign to provide Arab tanks with back-up lights.

* * *

"It's unfair," said a U.A.R. spokesman, "Israel has two million three hundred thousand Jews on her side. And we have none!"

Reports from the second day of fighting indicated that the Egyptians had destroyed four Jeeps, a kosher mobile kitchen, and fourteen air-conditioned Cadillacs.

The Israelis claimed four hundred MIGs and twenty-four flying carpets.

In Jerusalem two elderly men were sitting on a park bench discussing the war.

"How long do you think it will last?"

"Two months, the most!"

"So quick?"

"My son joined the Army and he never yet held a job for longer than two months in his life!"

* * *

SIGN IN ISRAELI BARRACKS
Privates Will Kindly Refrain from Giving Advice to Officers.

* * *

The air-raid siren went off in Haifa. A woman rushed down the stairs toward the basement. Suddenly she noticed that her husband had not followed her down. "Come on, Sidney," she yelled.

"Just a minute!" answered her husband. "I gotta get my teeth!"

"Never mind your teeth!" the wife shouted back. "What do you think they're dropping—pastrami sandwiches?"

* * *

A U.N. observer began chatting with an Israeli paratrooper. "How many successful jumps have you made?" asked the United Nations guard.

"Every one of the jumps was successful," said the Israeli. "I'm here!"

Yarkoni and Danberg, two Israeli soldiers, were bemoaning the years of hardship and fighting against the Egyptians.

"What we should do," suggested Yarkoni "is declare war against the United States. They'll beat us, and like they always do with all the countries they defeat, right away they'll give us billions of dollars, plenty of food, houses, cars, and factories."

"That's no good," sighed Danberg. "With our luck, *we'd* win!"

*　　*　　*

First Israeli soldier:	Don't worry, God will arrange it that Sadat will die on a Jewish holiday.
Second Israeli soldier:	How can you be sure?
First Israeli soldier:	Listen, any day that Sadat dies will be a Jewish holiday.

*　　*　　*

Moshe Dayan can't give back the captured Arab territories—they're all in his wife's name.

A group of American tourists was being shown around Tel Aviv. They arrived at the tomb of the Unknown Soldier. The guide pointed out the inscription at the bottom of the tomb:

HERE LIES ABRAHAM SCHWARTZ. BORN 1923. DIED 1973, DURING ARAB-ISRAELI WAR. A GOOD SOLDIER AND A GREAT FURRIER.

"What's all that fur business?" asked a surprised tourist. "This is supposed to be an unknown soldier."

"That's true," said the guide. "As a soldier nobody knew him, but as a furrier he was famous!"

*　　*　　*

Master storyteller Myron Cohen broke up "The Tonight Show" with this gem:

Vice-President Ford arrived in Israel and asked to see the Wailing Wall. Prime Minister Meir took him to the Wall, whereupon the Vice-President began to pray.

"Help Mr. Nixon guide our country!" He turned to Mrs. Meir and asked, "Is that nice?"

"That's nice!" she answered.

"Thank you for making me the Vice-President," he directed to the Wall. And then to the Prime Minister, "Is that nice?"

"That's nice," she replied.

"Let Israel give back the land they took from the Arabs so there will be peace in the Middle East . . . Is that nice?"

"You're talking to a wall!" said Mrs. Meir.

The following conversation was alleged to have taken place between the President of the United States and the Prime Minister of Israel:

Nixon: You have no idea how tough it is being President in a country with two hundred million citizens.

Meir: It's even tougher being a citizen in a country with two million Prime Ministers.

* * *

Kadish, a new immigrant to Israel, went to see the head of a government department for a job.

"What's your experience?" the official asked. "What can you do?"

"Nothing!" answered Kadish.

"Good!" said the civil servant. "Then we won't have to break you in!"

* * *

"Are there any golf courses in Israel?" asked a tourist of his guide.

"Think about it," his guide replied. "In a country as tiny as ours, a good drive could become an international incident!"

* * *

What's the fastest thing on earth?

An Arab riding a bicycle down Collins Avenue in Miami Beach.

Teitelbaum was taking his first jet plane ride. Nervous and on the verge of nausea, he had just buckled his seat belt when a huge Arab with long flowing robes sat down beside him.

After takeoff, the Arab immediately fell asleep and Teitelbaum yearned to visit the lavatory. He feared waking the sleeping giant beside him. Finally, Teitelbaum became so sick to his stomach that he threw up all over the Arab's beautiful robes.

Ten minutes later, the Arab awoke and was shocked to see the mess on his clothes. Teitelbaum smiled at him and said, "You feel better now?"

Overheard in New York's Garment District:

"I'm in favor of putting a statue of Sadat in the middle of Times Square."

"For what?"

"It'll give us shade in the summertime, shelter in the wintertime, and the birds a chance to speak for us all."

* * *

Rabbi Jacob Pressman of Temple Beth Am in Los Angeles tells about the French, English, and Israeli archeologists captured by two Arabs in the Sinai Desert.

"You dogs! We're going to kill you!"

"Vive la France!" shouted the Frenchman. "I'm ready!"

"God save the Queen!" proclaimed the Englishman. "Go ahead and shoot!"

"Punch me in the nose first!" begged the Israeli. And the Arabs pummeled him.

"Kick me in the behind!" said the Israeli.

"With pleasure!" answered the Arabs. And they did so with great relish.

"Now," said the Israeli, "hit me in the stomach!"

The Arabs pounded him to the ground. The Israeli then pulled out a gun and shot both Arabs dead.

"That was wonderful!" said the Englishman. "But why did you allow them to beat you so unmercifully?"

"If I'd shot them first," said the Israeli, "I would've been condemned as the aggressor!"

16

Prime Minister Indira Gandhi visited Israel and was welcomed by Golda Meir. After seeing all the historical sights, Mrs. Gandhi said, "I would like to visit a synagogue!"

"By all means!" answered the Israeli Prime Minister.

Two weeks later, Mrs. Gandhi stood before her Cabinet. "What did you learn in Israel?" asked one of the members.

"Many things!" answered the Indian Prime Minister. "But most of all I learned that in Israel synagogues, the men pray on the first floor and the Prime Ministers worship in the balcony!"

* * *

Two men meet in Palestine.
"Say, aren't you from New York?"
"Yes!"
"What's your name?"
"Riley!"
"*Riley?* What are you doing over here?"
"Living the life of Cohen!"

* * *

"Me, I blame everything on Moses!"
"What does he have to do with our troubles?"
"When Moses crossed the Red Sea, if he'd a made a left turn instead of a right, the Arabs would've gotten the sand and we would've gotten the oil."

George Jessel, renowned for his eulogies at funerals, was once ribbed by Jack Benny at a Friar's Roast:

"One of the nicest eulogies I ever heard Jessel deliver was for one of James Mason's cats. You just wouldn't believe what that cat had done for Israel!"

* * *

Ten minutes after the El Al jet left the Tel Aviv airport, a voice came over the loudspeaker:

"Good evening, this is your captain. I wanna wish you all a wonderful trip. God willing, we'll get you there safely. But God forbid we do have trouble, you'll find life belts under your seats. And if you have to put them on, God help us, you should wear them in the best of health!"

* * *

Milton Wildman, New Jersey stock market analyst, returned from a visit to Israel with this classic contribution:

Mrs. Lupowitz, an elderly widow newly arrived in the Holy Land, jumped into a public taxi traveling from Tel Aviv to Haifa. To the annoyance of the other five passengers, she kept reminding the driver, "Tell me when we pass Shefayim!"

Mrs. Lupowitz asked the driver so many times that the poor man drove right through Shefayim. When he realized his mistake, he apologized to the other occupants, turned the vehicle around, and drove back.

"Here is Shefayim!" said the driver. "Now you can get out!"

"Who wants to get out!" said Mrs. Lupowitz.

"You did!"

"No," said Mrs. Lupowitz. "My daughter told me when I left Tel Aviv that when I pass Shefayim, I should take my medicine."

* * *

SHMALTZ

Roses are red,
Violets are bluish.
If it wasn't for Christmas,
We'd all be Jewish.

*   *   *

Weinberg came home unexpectedly and found Mrs. Weinberg in bed with another man. "What the hell are you doing?" shouted the irate husband.

"See?" said his wife to the man beside her. "Didn't I tell you he was stupid?"

*   *   *

How can you tell the difference between a Jew and an Italian?
The Jew is the one in the Italian suit.

Paul Mosher, TV promotional giveaway king, got howls at a friend's dinner party with this switch on married life:

Mr. and Mrs. Blumstein stood outside the gorilla cage at the zoo. They gaped at the huge animal for a long time, unaware that the ape was staring at Mrs. Blumstein and becoming sexually aroused.

Suddenly, it became apparent that the gorilla had an erection. He reached through the bars, pulled Mrs. Blumstein into the cage, and began ripping off her clothes. "What should I do?" she screamed hysterically to her husband.

"Do what you do with me," replied Mr. Blumstein. "Tell him you got a headache!"

Newman went to Florida for his health, and two weeks later died of a heart attack. His body was shipped back to New York for the funeral. Two of Newman's friends came to see him as he lay in the casket.

"Doesn't he look wonderful?" said the first.

"Yeah," said the other. "Those two weeks in Florida sure did him a world of good!"

* * *

Rubin and Marcus, who were gin-rummy addicts, met one day in the country-club card room. Rubin had just learned that Marcus had been making love to his spouse.

"Look," said Rubin, "I know you've been foolin' around with my wife, but I still love her. So let's settle this in a civilized way."

"What do you want to do?" asked Marcus.

"I'll play you one game of gin; the winner gets to keep my wife!"

"Okay," agreed Marcus. "But just to make it interesting—let's play for a penny a point!"

* * *

JEWISH FAIRY
Heblew

In the state of New York, out on Long Island, there is a charming suburban town called Massapequa. There are so many Jewish and Italian residents in Massapequa that the city fathers are thinking of changing the name to Matzoh–Pizza.

* * *

Stern had just returned from a Florida vacation. "How was the weather?" asked a friend.

"It was so hot in Miami Beach," said Stern, "the women weren't wearing their mink stoles—just the appraisals!"

* * *

Mickey Katz, the ever-popular musician-comedian, fractures audiences with this one:

Silverstein, the inveterate joiner, came rushing home, proudly holding a membership card to his newest organization.

"Look," said Silverstein to his son, "I just joined the Prostitute Club!"

"What?" said the boy. "Let me see that card!" After reading it, he announced: "Pa, that's the Parachute Club!"

"All I know is," said Silverstein, "they guaranteed me three hundred sixty-five jumps a year!"

Mrs. Fleishman and Mrs. Rutkin were rocking on the porch of their Catskill Mountain hotel.

"Oh, my God!" exclaimed Mrs. Fleishman. "Look at that boy. Did you ever see such a big nose? Such a crooked mouth? And look—he's cockeyed too!"

"That," said Mrs. Rutkin, "happens to be my son!"

"Well," said Mrs. Fleishman, "on *him*, it's very becoming!"

* * *

Bob Mitchell, the exclusive wallpaper designer-manufacturer, tells about the Shoenfelds, who were upstairs in their bed.

"Wake up!" cried Mrs. Shoenfeld, nudging her husband. "There are burglars in the kitchen. I think they're eating the pot roast I made tonight!"

"What do we care," said Mr. Shoenfeld. "As long as they don't die in the house!"

* * *

By mistake, Rosenbloom walked into the women's locker room of an exclusive country club and started taking a shower. Suddenly, he heard female voices.

Realizing where he was, Rosenbloom wrapped a towel around his head and began walking toward the exit.

"Thank God!" gasped one lady, staring

at his nakedness intently. "It's not my husband!"

"He's not mine, either!" retorted the gal beside her.

"Girls," announced a third woman, "he's not even a member of the club!"

* * *

Irene Ginsburg, dynamic fund-raiser for the National Council of Jewish Women, heard this at one of her charity events:

Rosenfeld walked into the house with a grin on his face. "You'll never guess what a bargain I just got," he told his wife. "I bought four polyester, steel-belted, radial, wide-tread, whitewall, heavy-duty tires. On sale yet!"

"Are you nuts?" shrieked Mrs. Rosenfeld. "What did you buy tires for? You don't even have a car!"

"So?" said Rosenfeld. "You buy brassieres, don't you?"

* * *

"My name is Mortimer P. Quinn!"

"How do you spell Quinn?"

"C-o-h-e-n."

"What does the 'P' stand for?"

"The 'P' is silent, like in water!"

"There's no 'P' in water."

"I could see you was never swimming in Coney Island."

27

A German politician pleaded with Hitler not to mistreat the Jews. "If for no other reason," he said, "than just because they're so smart!"

"What makes you think the Jews are so smart?" asked the dictator.

"Come and I'll show you!"

He took the Nazi leader to Guttman's Gift Shop and said, "Ask him for a *left*-handed teapot."

The Führer did. Guttman went to the back of the store, picked up a teapot, turned it around, and returned.

"You're in luck," said Guttman, handing the teapot to Hitler. "I just happened to have one left!"

Back out on the street, the politician said, "You see, that's what I mean about the Jews being so smart!"

"What's so smart about that?" exclaimed Hitler. "He just happened to have one left!"

* * *

The whole world is Jewish. Even the sun is called Sol.

* * *

In the days of sailing ships men were often punished by whipping. And so it was that Swenson, Polski, and Rabinowitz were to be flogged for their misdeeds.

"Before I beat you," said the Captain to the Swede, "what do you want on your back?"

"I want some grease!" said Swenson.

After the flogging, the captain asked the same question of the Pole.

"I strong," said Polski. "I want nothing on my back!"

When the thirty lashes had been given, the captain said, "All right, Rabinowitz, what do you want on your back?"

"Well," said Rabinowitz, "I'd like to have that Polack on my back!"

* * *

Comedian Aloysius Bernie overheard this exchange in the cocktail lounge of the Concord Hotel:

Young man: Are you dancing?
Young woman: Are you asking?
Young man: I'm asking!
Young woman: I'm dancing!

* * *

WIFELY COMMENTS DURING
LOVEMAKING WITH HUSBAND

Italian: Oh, Gino, you are the world's greatest lover!

French: Ah, Jacques, my darling, you are marvelous! More! More!

Jewish: Oy, Jake, the ceiling needs painting!

Brotsky sent his only son to Europe to study the violin. Eight years later the boy returned, and Brotsky rented Carnegie Hall for his debut.

"If my son is a big hit," said Brotsky to all his relatives and friends, "we're gonna have a celebration party in the main ballroom of the Waldorf Astoria."

The big night arrived. The boy walked out on stage and was terrible. The violin squeaked. The strings broke. The audience was bored to death.

Brotsky, realizing the night was a gigantic failure, rushed over to the Waldorf to cancel the dinner. Sitting at a front table were three relatives, eating like crazy.

"What are you doing here?" shouted Brotsky. "I told you I'd have a party only if my son was a success!"

"Whaddaya want from us?" asked a fifth cousin. "*We* liked him!"

* * *

BAGEL
A doughnut dipped in cement

* * *

"Every girl I bring home, my mother doesn't like," said Norman to an old college chum. "They're either too tall or too short, too smart or too dumb, too fat or too thin, too loud or too quiet. I just can't seem to please her!"

"Just keep looking," said his friend, "till you find a girl who looks like your mother. Then she can't find fault with her!"

Three months later, Norman met his buddy again. "I did what you said," he announced. "I looked and I looked until I finally found a girl just like my mother. The same height, the same weight, the same personality, the same mind. She was exactly like my mother!"

"What happened?"

"My father hated her!"

* * *

Sidney Stevens, of Mannis Furs at Caesar's Palace in Las Vegas, overheard this conversation:

"Whatsa matter, Harry?"

"Ah, my wife is allergic to fur. Every time she sees another woman wearing a mink coat—she gets sick!"

* * *

Seymour telephoned his mother from London. "I didn't want you to think I forgot your birthday, Mama," he said. "I'm sending you a Picasso and a Jaguar!"

Three weeks later, he called again. "Did you get the two gifts I sent you?"

"I only got one!" answered his mother.

"Which one?"

"I don't know!"

Nils Shapiro, New York marketing exec, saw a crowd lining Riverside Drive to cheer Cardinal Spellman. Loudest of the cheerers was a little old Jewish lady, holding her granddaughter aloft to catch a glimpse of the passing prelate.

"It's very nice of you to get so excited over Cardinal Spellman!" observed Shapiro.

"Cardinal Spellman!" repeated the startled old lady. "I thought it was Mischa Elman!"

* * *

Maury Gidlow, sales champ for Carroll & Co. in Beverly Hills, came up with this classic:

Kotch and Wexler had just finished their lunch in a Lower East Side New York restaurant. "Tea or coffee, gentlemen?" asked the waiter.

"I'll have tea!" said Kotch.

"Me too!" said Wexler. "Make sure the glass is clean!"

The waiter left and returned in a few minutes with the order. "Two teas!" he announced. "Which one asked for a clean glass?"

* * *

Two ladies met at a Hadassah luncheon. "How's your daughter?" asked Mrs. Krantz.

"Oh-h, she's married to a prince!" boasted Mrs. Gottlieb. "He lets her sleep until eleven o'clock in the morning. She doesn't have to put her fingers in cold water. And all afternoon she does nothing but sip cocktails!"

"And what about your son?" asked Mrs. Krantz.

"Oh, I'm heartbroken," moaned Mrs. Gottlieb. "That poor boy is married to such a girl—she sleeps until eleven o'clock in the morning. She doesn't lift her fingers to put them in cold water! And what do you think? She's a *drunkard!* All afternoon she does nothing but sip cocktails!"

* * *

CATSKILLS HOTEL
Little Mandy Kornblum's Chateau in the Pussy Willows

* * *

Ann Dan, Los Angeles City School Coordinator, says she's absolutely certain that during a school celebration of Christmas, one of the children sang: "God rest ye, Jerry Mendelbaum!"

* * *

Milton Blackstone, Southern California special-events producer, provides this definition of a *bris**: "It's a small surgical procedure that we Jews have turned into a catered affair."

---

*circumcision ceremony

The Pharaoh decided to go for a ride up the Nile. "Captain of the Guards!" he shouted. "Get eighty Jewish slaves for oarsmen!"

Two hours later, the Egyptian leader was sailing up the river. In the hold, the Jews were rowing at a wicked pace.

Lieberman, the slaves' wit, turned to the rower beside him. "Tell me," said Lieberman, "on a cruise like this, how much do you tip the whipper?"

Lee Wolfberg, talent manager and raconteur, smiles when he thinks of an aunt who lived in Brooklyn. On his way East from Hollywood, Lee sent his relative a magnum of champagne and a pound of caviar.

When he arrived in New York, he phoned her. "Did you like the gift I sent you?"

"The ginger ale wasn't so bad. But that huckleberry jelly—you must've left it standing next to some fish in the icebox all night."

* * *

Comedian Dave Barry was driving along late one night and saw a sign: MENDELSOHN'S MOTEL. Underneath, it said: TV. Dave stopped at the place, got a room, and found there was no television set.

"There's a sign outside that says 'TV,'" Barry complained to the owner.

"Naturally," said Mendelsohn. "That means, *T*ourists *V*elcome!"

* * *

Sokolow: I just got a beautiful French poodle for my wife.
Neiman: Tell me, how did you make such a good trade?

* * *

Mushkin was visiting a cemetery and noticed a magnificent marble mausoleum.

Above the doorway was chiseled: ROTH-SCHILD.

"Oh, boy!" said Mushkin. "Now, that's what I call living!"

* * *

Jack Lewerke, California record promoter, convulsed poker pals with this modern-day mother story:

Ira quit college, got himself a back pack, and began hitchhiking around the United States. After he had been gone more than a year, he telephoned home.

"Hello, Ma, how are you?"

"Just fine, son. When're you coming home? I'll fix you some chopped liver and chicken soup and a beautiful pot roast!"

"I'm still pretty far away!"

"Oh, son!" cried the desperate woman. "Just come home and I'll fix your favorite —oatmeal cookies!"

"I don't like oatmeal cookies!" said the boy.

"You don't?" asked the woman.

"Say," said Ira, "is this Century 5-7682?"

"No!"

"Then I must have the wrong number!"

"Does that mean you're not coming?" asked the woman.

* * *

SHTICK

Mat-zoh[1]: Temporary filling for tooth cavities.

Mish-poch-eh[2]: Foreign relations committee.

Zay-dah[3]: Grandchild's press agent.

Mach-ay-eh[4]: Finding a quarter in a phone booth.

Taka a mach-ay-eh[5]: Japanese sex relations.

Hal-vah[6]: Kasha dipped in cement.

Bar Mitzvah[7]: Jewish dude ranch.

---

[1]*unleavened bread* [2]*family* [3]*grandfather* [4]*good feeling* [5]*heavenly feeling* [6]*Turkish candy* [7]*ceremony held when a boy reaches the age of thirteen*

39

Far-blund-jet[8]: Owning a kosher butcher shop in Cairo.

Far-ga-nigen[9]: Front table at a nudie show.

Fay-ga-leh[10]: A man who likes to take another man to lunch and *he* is the lunch.

Yen-tah[11]: The FBI in bloomers.

Shad-chen[12]: A man who knows the perfect girl for you—and married the wrong girl himself.

Schle-miel[13]: A man who takes a bath and forgets to wash his face.

Shik-eh[14]: Jewish Dean Martin.

Shik-seh[15]: A woman who does all her own housework.

Shay-gitz[16]: A guy who thinks a *shikseh* is an electric razor.

Cocker: A diarrhetic diabetic.

Alta cocker: (a) An old man overdosed with milk of magnesia.
  (b) One who fires blanks.
Shmonk: A rabbi who lives in a monastery.

---

[8]*extremely confused* [9]*real happiness* [10]*homosexual*
[11]*gossipy woman* [12]*marriage broker* [13]*simpleton* [14]*drunk*
[15]*gentile woman* [16]*gentile man*

SHMATTES

"The dress business is so bad," complained Hockman, "this last year I've been losing eight hundred dollars a week. And that's week after week after week!"

"So why don't you give up the business?"

"So how am I gonna make a living?"

*   *   *

"Is your son a good businessman?" asked Jaffe.

"My boy is so dedicated to his work," said Isaacs, "that he keeps his secretary near his bed in case he should get an idea during the night!"

*   *   *

SIGN IN WINDOW OF BANKRUPT
STORE
We Undersold Everybody

Sol (telephoning his partner from Miami):
    How's everything in New York?
Eli: Everything's all right.
Sol: How's the weather?
Eli: How should the weather be?
Sol: How's business in the shop?
Eli: It's fine but I got bad news for you.
Sol: Whatsa matta?
Eli: We've been robbed!
Sol: Don't be silly, Eli! Put it back!

Levy closed his shop Friday night and headed for temple services, not realizing his fly was unzipped. At the entrance, he met Mrs. Weiss, the president of the Ladies' Auxiliary. "I don't like to say nothin'," she said shyly, "but your business is open!"

"You're mistaken, lady!" said Levy.

"Believe me," said Mrs. Weiss, blushing, "your business is open!"

"You're crazy!" shouted Levy, rushing inside. "I close the store every Friday to come here!"

Later, at home, Levy saw that his fly was open and realized that Mrs. Weiss had only been trying to tell him so in a delicate way. He telephoned her immediately.

"I wanna apologize!" he said, also trying to be tactful. "But tell me somethin'. When my business was open, was my salesman in or out?"

* * *

This past season in New York, business was so bad the dress manufacturers were firing their sons-in-law.

* * *

Comedy star Jackie Kahane broke up a Jewish benefit audience with this one:

Fligelman's jewelry store was held up. The owner telephoned the police, and a squad car arrived immediately.

"You wouldn't believe it!" cried Fligelman to the first cop. "I was robbed by an elephant!"

"By a *what?*" asked the policeman.

"An elephant!" exclaimed the shopkeeper. "A big truck pulled up in front of the store, an elephant got out, he gave the window a knock with his trunk, broke the glass, took all the jewelry, and left."

"An elephant from India has short ears," said the officer, "and an African elephant has long ears. What kind was it?"

"How the hell do I know?" screamed Fligelman. "He had a stocking over his head!"

*   *   *

TV producer Perry Cross tells this beaut to special friends:

As in most businesses, nepotism is very much part of the motion picture industry. At one time, the head of a large studio brought in the boy who had married his daughter and made him production chief.

Within six months, the young man produced three pictures that were financial disasters. The father-in-law called the boy into his office.

"It's not bad enough," he screamed, "the movies you made were lousy. And that you lost millions of dollars. But you set the son-in-law business back twenty years!"

"Jake, you took your son-in-law into the dress business with you, how's he doin'?"

"It's amazing," said Jake. "He's been with me now only two weeks and already he's a month behind in his work!"

*　　*　　*

Lubin and Weber met on Seventh Avenue. "How's business?" asked Lubin.

"Lousy!" answered Weber. "On Monday, the whole day, I sold only one suit. Tuesday, business was so bad, the salesmen were trying to sell each other. And Wednesday was even worse, yet. The man that bought the suit Monday brought it back!"

*　　*　　*

Comedian London Lee, who came from a wealthy manufacturing family, kids about it. "The nicest thing about money," says London, "is that it never clashes with anything you're wearing!"

*　　*　　*

Furriers Raskin and Miller met in Miami. "You took your son, the college boy, into the business. How's he working out?"

"You wouldn't believe it!" replied Miller. "He wants to cross mink with kangaroo to get fur coats with pockets in them!"

* * *

Gene McGarr, TV and motion picture director, tells about Bercovitz and Michelson, who were not only business partners but lifelong friends. They made a pact that whichever one died first, he would come back and tell the other what it was like in Heaven.

Six months later, Bercovitz died. And Michelson waited for his dear, departed friend to show some sign that he had returned to earth. Michelson passed the time impatiently hoping for and eagerly awaiting a message from Bercovitz.

Then, one year after the day of his death, Bercovitz spoke to Michelson. It was late at night. Michelson was in bed.

"Michelson! Michelson!" echoed a voice.

"Is that you, Bercovitz?"

"Yes!"

"What is it like where you are?"

"We have breakfast and then we screw. Then we eat lunch and we screw. We have dinner and then we screw!"

"Is that what Heaven is like?" asked Michelson.

"Who said anything about Heaven?" said Bercovitz. "I'm in Wisconsin and I'm a bull!"

Stan Wanderman, prez of Sunday's Child, the California dress firm, overheard this conversation at the L.A. Merchandise Mart:

"Did you hear what Melnick did with his secretary?"

"No!"

"Well, he'd been trying to make out with her for months but she kept turning him down!"

"So?"

"So, he stapled her tits together!"

"What?"

"Yeah, Melnick says his motto is: 'If you can't lick 'em—join 'em!' "

* * *

Berger and Baum were partners. While they were having lunch, Berger shouted: "Oh, my God!"

"Whatsa matta?" asked Baum.

"We went away," said Berger, "and we left the safe open!"

"Whatta you worried?" asked his partner. "We're both here!"

* * *

Irv Robbins, the brilliant guiding hand behind Baskin-Robbins, the ice cream America loves, tells about the manufacturer who phoned a friend.

"Sy, I'm in big trouble. I'm about to go bankrupt—unless I can raise some cash—and I haven't the slightest idea where I'm going to get it from."

"I'm glad to hear it," said his friend. "For a minute there I was afraid you might think you could borrow it from me!"

* * *

Rosenbaum sold hot dogs from a push-cart. "How's business?" asked an acquaintance.

"Could be worse!" said Rosenbaum. "I put away already two thousand dollars in the bank!"

"That's good," said the friend. "Maybe you could lend me five dollars?"

"I'm not allowed!"

"What *not allowed*?"

"I made an agreement with the bank. They agreed not to sell hot dogs if I promised I wouldn't make loans!"

* * *

Schecter rented space at one of those outdoor California swap meets. A woman customer picked up a broken fork and asked, "How much?"

"A penny," said Schecter.

"A penny!" grumbled the woman. "That's too much!"

"So make me an offer."

* * *

Krebs ran into Fink on Broadway. "Hey," cried Krebs, "I heard you had a fire!"

"Ssh!" said Fink. "It's not till next week!"

Sakolski got a job driving a bus. At the end of the first day he turned in the receipts—$58. The next day's returns were $61. On the third day, he brought in $56. But on the fourth day, Sakolski gave the cashier $243.

"This is great!" exclaimed the cashier. "That route never brought in that much money. What happened?"

"After three days on that lousy route," explained Sakolski, "I figured business wasn't gonna get any better, so I drove over to Broadway and worked there. Say, that street is a regular gold mine!"

* * *

Levine and Friedman, two garment workers, were strolling through Central Park one sunny spring afternoon.

"Look at them gorgeous flowers!" remarked Levine. "Are they daisies?"

"How should I know?" snapped Friedman. "I'm not in millinery!"

* * *

Joel Davis, National Media Consultants V.P., tells about Cohen and Goldberg, who were partners in the dress business. And business was terrible! A discouraged Cohen announced to his partner that he was going to change his name for good luck.

"From now on," he said, "I'm O'Brien."

That night Goldberg decided he would change his name, too. Both men instructed the switchboard operator to answer the phones: "O'Brien and O'Brien!"

Everything went fine until a caller demanded to speak to Mr. O'Brien.

"Which O'Brien do you want?" asked the operator. "Cohen or Goldberg?"

* * *

"I can't understand it," said Bloom to his partner, Rifkin. "Here we are bankrupt, through, findished—and only yesterday the President said that business was booming!"

"Maybe," said Rifkin, "the President has a better location!"

* * *

New York film producer–author Bud Greenspan remembers this classic:

Jacobs the junk peddler was trudging wearily through New York's Lower East Side one hot summer day. On his shoulder, Jacobs carried a large canvas bag loaded with iron, lead pipe, and brass that he had collected.

Jacobs, perspiring freely was making very slow progress with the heavy bag. Suddenly, a woman in a fifth-story window attracted his attention.

"Mister!" she called. "Come on up!"

Slowly, the old man climbed the four flights of stairs and finally got to the fifth floor. "Now," said the woman, "you tell little Bernard if he ain't a good boy you're gonna put him in that bag and take him away!"

Saul Budd of New York's Home Curtain Company contributed this doozy:

Rothstein owed a hundred dollars to Weiner. The debt was past due and Rothstein was broke, so he borrowed the hundred dollars from Spivak and paid Weiner.

A week later, Rothstein borrowed back the hundred dollars from Weiner and paid Spivak. Another week went by and Rothstein borrowed back the hundred dollars from Spivak to pay Weiner.

He repeated this transaction several times, until finally he called them up and said, "Fellas, this is a lotta bother. Why don't you two exchange the hundred dollars every week and keep me out of it!"

Mrs. Glick phoned the president of Macy's at four A.M. and said, "I just want to tell you how much I like the hat I bought!"

"That's very nice, madam!" said the executive. "But why did you have to wake me at four o'clock in the morning just to tell me that!"

"Because they just delivered it!" said Mrs. Glick.

* * *

Morty Bass, of Jeri Morton, Inc., New York's leading lingerie manufacturer, came up with this perfect solution to handling business:

In a small village in Russia, a marriage broker was trying to arrange a match between a beautiful young girl and Fishbach, a businessman. But Fishbach was stubborn. "Before I buy goods from a mill," he said, "I look at swatches. Before I get married, I gotta have a sample also."

"But my God!" exclaimed the marriage broker. "You can't ask a decent, respectable girl for a thing like that!"

"I am a businessman," said Fishbach, "and that's the way it's gonna be done!"

The broker went off sadly to talk to the girl. "I've got a fine fella for you," he began. "Lotsa money. A-one rating. But he's a little eccentric. He says he's a good businessman and he won't go into anything blind. He insists on a sample."

"Listen," said the girl, "I'm as good a businessman as he is. Samples, I wouldn't give him. But I will give him references!"

* * *

Kravitz had a heart attack. He was still a young man, but the doctors warned him not to work. "I don't know what we're gonna do," he said to his wife.

"Don't worry, sweetheart," said Mrs. Kravitz. "I can work!"

"But you've never held a job in your life! We've got thousands of dollars worth of bills."

"I could make the money as a streetwalker!"

Before Kravitz could object, his wife rushed out the door. She returned that night and placed fifty dollars and ten cents on the table.

"Who the hell gave you a dime?" shrieked Kravitz.

"Everybody!" said his wife.

* * *

Steve Sheldon, Beverly Hills talent manager, tells about the two dress-firm partners:

"You bastard!" shouted Max. "You've been sleeping with my wife!"

"Honest, Max!" said his partner. "Not a wink!"

Will Marks, the New Jersey auto-body repair mogul, passed us this favorite:

Business partners Slodnick and Weinstock wanted to hire a new secretary.

"Well," said Slodnick, "you saw the three girls I just interviewed. A blonde, a brunette, and a redhead. They're all equally competent. Which one should we hire?"

"I think," announced Weinstock, "we should hire the one with the big titties!"

*   *   *

Stanley Ralph Ross, the celebrated Hollywood screenwriter-author and raconteur, tells about Mishkin, the dress salesman who covered the Midwest.

His first stop was Chicago. Mishkin checked into a hotel. In the middle of the night the place caught fire. Mishkin came running out on the street with nothing on—except an erection.

He stopped one of the firemen. "When you go inside," said Mishkin, "if you see a gorgeous redhead with big boobies and a nice behind, give her a screw—it's paid for already!"

*   *   *

In a New York City night court, three girls charged with soliciting on the street, and Liebowitz, arrested for peddling ties without a license, were brought before the judge.

"This is all a mistake, Your Honor," said the first harlot. "I was walkin' along and this guy—"

"Just a minute, young lady," said the judge. "You've been here a dozen times. One hundred dollars fine. Next!"

"I'm just a poor private secretary," said the second girl, "and I wasn't doing anything—"

"I recognize you too, miss," said the magistrate. "Two hundred dollars or ten days in jail. Next case!"

"Judge," said the third girl. "I'm a prostitute! I'm not proud of it, but it's the only way I can support my three kids. I'm guilty!"

"Young woman," said the judge, "I like your honesty. And because of it, I'm going to give you a break. Your case is dismissed. And Sergeant, give this girl fifty dollars out of the Policemen's Fund!"

Now comes poor old Liebowitz, arrested for selling ties without a license. "Your Honor," he pleaded, "I'm not gonna lie to you. I'm a prostitute!"

* * *

Comedienne Joan Rivers broke up the audience on the Johnny Carson show when she told about her high-school friend, Heidi Abramowitz.

Heidi was the school pushover. Joan met her ten years later and said, "Heidi, what are you up to?"

"Fifty dollars!" said her school chum.

Jake! I heard you had a big fire at the store!

Ssh! It's not until next weekend.

*   *   *

Cooperman sold strawberries off his truck out in the suburbs. He knocked on the door of a house. "Wanna buy some strawberries?"

"Come around back!" answered the pretty young blonde.

Cooperman walked to the rear, rang the bell, and the woman opened the door. To Cooperman's shock, she stood there stark naked. Not a stitch of clothes on. Cooperman started to cry.

"What's the matter?" asked the blonde.

"Today, my wife ran away with my best friend," explained Cooperman, "I lost three thousand dollars on the stock market, and now you're gonna *screw* me out of my strawberries!"

* * *

Tillie and Minnie, two old girl friends, met for lunch. "I married a wealthy clothing manufacturer," announced Tillie, "and he bought me a yacht for my birthday!"

"Astounding!" said Minnie.

"I have charge accounts in all the department stores!"

"Astounding!"

"I have a drawer full of rubies and emeralds and he bought me a twenty-five-carat diamond ring for our second anniversary!"

"Astounding!"

"What have you been doing?" asked Tillie.

"Oh," answered her friend, "going to charm school!"

"Really? What did you learn there?"

"They taught me to say 'astounding' instead of 'bullshit'!"

* * *

SHMOOZE

Yetta and Bessie, both grandmothers, were sitting on the sand in Miami Beach. "Isn't that ocean big?" said Yetta, gazing out at the Atlantic.

"Yeah," said Bessie, "and we're only looking at the top!"

* * *

Fein and Klein were sitting on a park bench. "I'll tell you the truth," said Fein, "I'm afraid to fly. Those airplanes ain't too safe!"

"Don't be a baby," said Klein, "Didn't you read last week there was a big train crash and three hundred people were killed!"

"Three hundred killed on a train—what happened?"

"An airplane fell on it!"

Smulowitz, aged eighty-three and widowed, refused to be placed in just any Miami Beach old-age home. "I won't eat anything," he declared to his son, "unless it's strictly kosher!"

The son searched for weeks and finally found a place that served meals in accordance with the Jewish dietary laws. He placed Smulowitz in the home, secure in the knowledge that his father would be eating only kosher food.

Three days later, he came for a visit and learned that the old man had left and checked into the Fontainebleau Hotel. The boy rushed over to the hotel, got a key, went upstairs, opened the door, and there was his father in bed with a blonde. They were both stark naked.

"Papa, how could you?" asked the bewildered boy.

"But look," said Smulowitz, "I'm not eating!"

Slutsky, eighty-five, was complaining to Blustein. "My housekeeper," he said, "is suing me for breach of promise!"

"At your age," inquired Blustein, "what could you promise her?"

*　　*　　*

Yetta: What's wrong with your hair, sweetheart? It looks like a wig!

Bessie: You know something, it *is* a wig!

Yetta: How do you like that—you never could tell!

*　　*　　*

Since many senior citizens have migrated to Florida, Yiddish theater has once again begun to flourish in Miami Beach. One night during a performance, the curtain suddenly came down and the stage manager stood before the audience.

"I'm sorry," he said, "but we have to stop the show. The leading man just died!"

After a gasp from the crowd, a little old lady in the balcony shouted, "Give him an enema!"

"Madam, maybe you didn't hear me! The man is dead!"

"Give him an enema!" she yelled again.

"Are you crazy or something?" retorted the stage manager. "The man is dead. An enema couldn't help him!"

"It couldn't hurt!"

Bessie: You know, before you turn
around, it'll be summer again.
Yetta: So don't turn!

* * *

Grandma Weinstein was walking through the park with two little boys when she met a friend. "How old are your grandchildren?" asked the woman.

"The doctor is five and the lawyer is seven!" answered Mrs. Weinstein proudly.

* * *

Mrs. Goldstein had been a widow for some time. One day she walked into a photo shop and said to the owner, "I'd like to have this picture of my poor dead husband fixed up!"

"What is it you want done?" asked the proprietor.

"Well, this picture is the only one that I have of him, but he's wearing a hat," explained the widow. "I want you should take off the hat so I could see his gorgeous hair!"

"What kind of hair did he have?"

"Take off the hat and you'll see!" replied Mrs. Goldstein.

* * *

JEWISH GERITOL
Chicken soup spiked with Manoschewitz

Yetta: If it was summer again, where would you go on a vacation?

Bessie: Well, last year we took a trip around the world. This year we would like to go somewhere different!

* * *

Senior citizens Israel and Emma met at a singles dance on Miami Beach, and within two weeks they were married. They felt it was a perfect match, for they were both ninety years old.

On the first night of their honeymoon, they got into bed and the old man squeezed Emma's hand. She squeezed back and they fell asleep.

The second night, Israel squeezed her hand again. Emma squeezed back and they went right to sleep.

On the third night, Israel once more squeezed his bride's hand. "Not tonight," said Emma, "I've got a headache!"

* * *

"My wife and me enjoyed Japan," said Fogel to his neighbor, Goodman, reminiscing about their forty-fifth wedding anniversary trip.

"What was so terrific?" asked Goodman.

"The first night we saw a Japanese girl do her Kabuki dance," explained Fogel. "And when she danced, I could actually see her Kabuki!"

Comedian George Kirby gets howls with this one:

Mrs. Weissman had her portrait painted. When it was finished, the artist presented it to her. "How do you like it?" he asked.

"It's nice!" answered Mrs. Weissman. "But I want you should add a gold bracelet on each wrist. A pearl necklace, ruby earrings, an emerald tiara, and on each finger I want you to put a twenty-carat diamond ring!"

"But," said the bewildered artist, "why do you want to ruin a good picture with all those gaudy trinkets?"

"My husband is running around with a young chippie," explained Mrs. Weissman, "and when I die, I want her to go crazy looking for the jewelry!"

*　　*　　*

Yetta: Tell me sweetheart, what do you think of sex?

Bessie: Well, I think it's the finest department store in New York!

*　　*　　*

"Is your grandfather a religious man?" asked the young coed of her date.

"He's so Orthodox," replied the boy, "When he plays chess, he doesn't use bishops—he uses rabbis."

69

Lovable Jack Barry, host of TV's "The Joker's Wild," recalls an incident early in his career. He was interviewing Mr. and Mrs. Blumenthal on their sixtieth wedding anniversary.

"How old is your wife?" asked Jack.

"She's eighty-seven," said Blumenthal, "and God willing, she'll live to be a hundred!"

"And how old are you?" inquired Barry.

"I'm eighty-seven too," answered the octogenarian, "and God willing, I'll live to be a hundred and one!"

"But why," asked Jack, "would you want to live a year longer than your wife?"

"To tell you the truth," said Blumenthal, "I'd like to have at least one year of peace!"

*   *   *

Yetta: I've been married over forty years and I'm gettin' a little itchy. How do you start an affair?

Bessie: I don't have too much experience in that . . . but I usually start an affair with "The Star Spangled Banner."

*   *   *

Mrs. Markowitz was walking along the beach with her grandson when suddenly a wave came and washed the three-year-old boy out to sea.

"Oh, Lord!" cried the woman. "If you'll

70

just bring that boy back alive I'll do anything. I'll be the best person. I'll give to charity. I'll go to temple. Please, God! Send him back!"

At that moment, a wave washed the child back up on the sand, safe and sound. His grandmother looked at the boy and then up to the heavens.

"Okay!" she exclaimed. "So where's his hat?"

* * *

Bert Goldberg, prez of Texas Joyce Bertram Bath Shops chain, tells about senior citizen Berkowitz crossing Washington Avenue on Miami Beach. The elderly man was hit by a passing auto. Several passersby picked him up and laid him down on a bench.

A kindly silver-haired matron approached the injured man and said, "Are you comfortable?"

"Eh! I make a living!" sighed Berkowitz.

* * *

A first-time visitor to Honolulu approached the gray-haired clerk at the airport newsstand. "You look like a native," said the woman. "What is the correct way to pronounce the name of your state? Is it Hawaii or Havaii?"

"Havaii!" answered the old man.

"Thank you!"

"You're velcome!"

Four women were chatting while playing Mah-Jongg. Each took a turn bragging about her children. When three of them had finished, Mrs. Hurowitz began.

"Ladies," she said, "you don't know what it means to have a good son. My boy lives in a penthouse and he built three rooms with a kitchen especially for me. He takes me out to dinner every night. We go to the theater three times a week. Last month he took me with him on vacation to Puerto Rico. He don't do nothing without talking to me first.

"And ladies," added Mrs. Hurowitz, "my son goes to a psychiatrist five times a week. And who do you think he spends the whole time talking about? Me!"

* * *

Yetta: You know something, sweetheart? I don't like to brag, but I've been to Europe three times already.
Bessie: So what? I was *born* there!

* * *

To celebrate their thirtieth wedding anniversary, Solomon came home and presented his wife with a little monkey.

"Are you crazy or somethin'??" shouted Mrs. Solomon. "Where the hell are we gonna keep a monkey?"

"Don't worry," said Solomon, "he'll sleep right in the bed with us!"

"And what about the smell?"

"If I could stand it for thirty years—he'll get used to it also!"

* * *

When George Gershwin became successful he brought his immigrant father to California. One day the senior Gershwin, who spoke English with a heavy accent, was stopped by a motorcycle cop for speeding.

"You can't give me a ticket," declared Papa Gershwin. "My son is Chudge Gershwin!"

"Okay," said the cop, "I'll just give you a warning this time." As he drove away he shouted, "And give my regards to the judge!"

* * *

Two senior citizens in Miami were chatting. "Fishman is eighty-six," said the first man, "and he has sex relations with his wife twice a week!"

"Don't believe it!" said the second man.

"All right, ask Mrs. Fishman and her three brothers. They're always there."

"Why are her three brothers always there?"

" 'Cause Fishman fights!"

Abramson had reached the grand old age of eighty and decided to celebrate. All his life he'd been Orthodox: worn a long beard, black hat, black suit, and black overcoat.

Now, to celebrate his birthday, the octogenarian shaved off the beard. He replaced his somber black clothes with the latest-style green-checked suit, a burgundy tie, and blue striped shirt, and headed for a massage parlor. As Abramson crossed the street he was struck by a truck and killed.

In Heaven, he spoke to his Maker. "God, why me? I was a good husband! I gave to all the charities. I've always been a religious man. Why me?"

"To tell the truth," said the Lord, "I didn't *recognize* you!"

* * *

Yetta: What do you think—the truth, now—what do you think about LSD?

Bessie: I think he was a wonderful President.

* * *

Mrs. Greenfield walked into a butcher shop and said to the owner, "If you'll be so kind, I'd like you should give me a half-dozen lamb chops. How much it's gonna cost?"

"For *you*," said the butcher, "two dollars and forty cents a pound!"

"Are you crazy?" shrieked Mrs. Greenfield. "I could get across the street by Schwartz for two dollars a pound!"

"So what're you bothering me?" bellowed the butcher. "Go buy your lamb chops from Schwartz!"

"He ain't got any!"

"Listen, if I wouldn't have any," said the butcher, "I'd sell you them for a dollar forty a pound!"

* * *

Bedraggled, worried Garfinkel sat in a train holding a three-year-old boy. Every few minutes Garfinkel spanked the child.

"If you strike that baby one more time," said a woman sitting across from him, "I'll give you so much trouble you won't forget it!"

"Trouble?" said Garfinkel. "You're gonna give me trouble? Lady, my partner stole all my money and ran off with my wife and car. My daughter's in the parlor car, six months pregnant, and she ain't got no husband. My baggage is lost, I'm on the wrong train, and this little stinker just ate the tickets and threw up all over me, And lady, *you're* gonna give me trouble?"

* * *

Yetta: What d'ya think—my husband came home yesterday and told me he bought a condominium!

Bessie: That's nice! But if I was you, I would still take the pill!

When Morganstein had reached the age of sixty-five, he suddenly began chasing the young chicks. A neighbor brought his behavior to the attention of his wife. "Whatta you gonna do about it?" she asked.

"Who cares?" said Mrs. Blumenthal. "Let him chase girls! Dogs chase cars—but when they catch them, they can't drive!"

Al Jolson used to tell this one about his father. "I bought my dad an overcoat that cost a couple hundred bucks. It was beautiful! But I knew the old guy'd say two hundred dollars was too much to spend for a coat. So I told him it only cost ten dollars.

"Three weeks later, he phoned me and said, 'That overcoat was some buy for ten dollars. I sold it to your uncle Max for twenty dollars. Send me a dozen more!' "

* * *

Three grandmothers playing cards poolside at the Eden Roc in Miami Beach were joined by a fourth.

"Sit down, darling!" said the leader of the group. "We're happy you should join us. We have certain rules while we're playing. *First,* we don't talk about our children. We all got sons, doctors, lawyers . . .

"*Second,* we don't talk about our grandchildren. We all got gorgeous grandchildren.

"And *third,* we don't talk about sex! What *was,* was!"

* * *

"If we was rich," said Mrs. Aaron, "we would spend six months a year in Florida, six months in California, and six months in Europe."

"But," said Mrs. Lasky, "that makes eighteen months in one year!"

"Ain't it grand what you could do with money?"

* * *

An elderly woman climbed three flights of stairs, opened a carved mahogany door and walked into a exotically furnished reception room. A gong sounded and out of a cloud of incense appeared a beautiful brunette Oriental.

"Do you," she said softly, "wish to meet with His Omnipotence, the wise, all-knowing, all-seeing guru, Maharishi Naru?"

"Yeah," said the gray-haired woman. "Tell Sheldon his mother is here from the Bronx!"

* * *

"Lieberman must be well on in age!"

"Yes, poor man! He's so old he gets winded playing checkers!"

* * *

Yetta: What would you do if you found a million dollars?

Bessie: Well, if it was a *poor person* that lost it, I'd give it back!

For centuries, European Jews were the victims of organized persecution, called pogroms. These pogroms took place so often that Jews developed a sense of humor about them.

In a small town in Poland, soldiers broke into the house of Ostrovsky and his family. Living with him were his wife, three daughters, two sons, and his aged mother.

"Line up!" shouted the sergeant in charge. "We're gonna beat up all the men and rape all the women!"

"Wait!" pleaded Ostrovsky. "You can wallop me and my sons, abuse my wife and daughters, but please sir, I beg you . . . don't rape my mother! She's seventy-five years old!"

"Shut up!" yelled the old woman. "A pogrom is a pogrom!"

Mrs. Goldfarb walked into a kosher butcher shop, asked the owner for a "fresh chicken," and immediately began inspecting it. She lifted the wing, stuck her nose underneath, and declared, "Phew! It smells!"

Then she pulled up a leg, sniffed and said, "Feh!"

After smelling the hind end, Mrs. Goldfarb held her nose and exclaimed, "It stinks! You call this a fresh chicken!"

"Tell me, lady," said the butcher, "you could stand such an inspection?"

*   *   *

Bernstein, anxious for a relaxing steam bath at the Turkish baths, could not get in because it was ladies' night. Undaunted, he went to a costume shop, rented a dress and wig, and entered the baths.

Draped in a sheet, Bernstein headed for the steam room. However, unbeknownst to him, the lower half of his sheet caught on a nail, exposing his body from the waist down.

A sweet, white-haired, woman stopped him and said, "I beg your pardon, madam! But your baby's leg is sticking out!"

*   *   *

Feingold, on his deathbed, was surrounded by his children. "Don't worry, Papa, we'll have a big funeral," declared his eldest son. "There'll be a hundred limousines, ten cars with flowers—"

"We don't need all that!" interrupted Feingold's second son. "Fifty limos and five cars with flowers is more than enough!"

"Whatta ya makin' such a big deal?" said the dying man's youngest son. "We don't need any flowers. We'll just have the immediate family! Two cars is enough!"

At that moment, Feingold raised himself up and said, "Listen, boys! Just hand me my pants and I'll *walk* to the cemetery!"

* * *

Two partners, Abrams and Schneider, agreed that whoever died first, the other one was to put five thousand dollars in the coffin. Abrams died, and Schneider fulfilled his part of the contract. He put in a check.

* * *

Meyer: I heard your father passed away.
Israel: Yeah, he died and left me four thousand dollars to buy a stone to remember him by.
Meyer: Isn't that a new diamond ring you're wearing?
Israel: Yeah, that's the stone I bought to remember him by.

Yetta: Well, goodbye, sweetheart! If I
live, I'll see you Wednesday!
Bessie: Okay.
Yetta: If not, Thursday!

* * *

Actor-comedian Jesse White tells about
the apartment house in the Bronx occupied
entirely by Jewish tenants. McMurphy was
the janitor.

"How do you like working here?" asked
Wasserman, one of the building's occupants.

"Oh, I love working for the Jews!" said
McMurphy. "In fact, I'll tell you a little
secret. I've made love to every woman in
this building—except one!"

Wasserman rushed upstairs. "You know
what the janitor just told me," he exclaimed to Mrs. Wasserman. "He's made
love to every woman in this building except one!"

"Well," said his wife, "it must be that
stuck-up Mrs. Rudnick on the second
floor!"

* * *

SHTOOPS

Flinging epithets at one's enemies is a time-honored device to vent anger and frustration. But Jews throughout the centuries developed the knack of framing contemptuous word pictures into a fine art.

As with all phrases taken from another language, these expletives lose something in the translation from their original Yiddish. Nevertheless, here are some classic Jewish curses:

You should only starve for a piece of bread and come to me for help and I should be too poor to help you!

* * *

All your teeth should fall out except one and that should have a toothache.

* * *

There should grow in your stomach a trolley car and I should be the conductor going, "Clang! Clang! Clang!"

You should live the rest of your life like a chandelier! You should hang all day and burn all night.

May you become a widower before your wife's death.

If you don't live to be an old maid, may you live to be a young widow.

May your wife be a witch who takes after her mother, and may you all live together in a one-room house.

You should grow like an onion, with your head in the ground and you feet in the air.

May the fleas from a thousand camels infest your armpits.

You should inherit a big house that has a thousand rooms and each room should have a featherbed and you should have a fever of 105 that should toss you from one bed to another and another and another!

Beets should only grow from your stomach and you should only pee borscht.

The fountain pen you gave me for Chanukah—it should only run from your nose like it leaks in my pocket.

You should have ten penthouses in ten Park Avenue buildings and in each one you should have a gorgeous blonde waiting to do your every wish and in front of each of these ten buildings you should have a Rolls Royce with a chauffeur and every morning you should get into each car and your chauffeur should drive you to a different doctor and not one doctor should know what's wrong with you!

* * *

SHOCHETS

What word beginning with "A" means "prince" in Jewish?
A doctor!

* * *

A psychiatrist and a proctologist became good friends and agreed to share offices to cut down on expenses. To economize even further, they had just one sign printed:
Dr. Marvin Hornstein, *Psychiatrist*
Dr. David Slodnick, *Proctologist*
SPECIALIZING IN ODDS AND ENDS

* * *

Dr. Arnold Epstein, Beverly Hills heart surgeon, gave this advice to a complaining hospital intern: "You can become a millionaire and immortal at the same time. All you have to do is invent a cure for which there is no disease."

After taking off her clothes for an examination, Mrs. Greenberg sat on the table. "Lady," said the doctor, "I have to tell you that you are by far the dirtiest, filthiest, most unclean woman I have ever examined in my life!"

"How d'ya like that!" said Mrs. Greenberg. "The doctor I went to yesterday said the same thing!"

"Then why did you come here?"

"I wanted to get another opinion!" answered Mrs. Greenberg.

"Your cousin's a famous surgeon?"

"A genius! He's the kind of a doctor, if you're at death's door—he'll pull you through!"

* * *

JEWISH PENICILLIN
Chicken soup

* * *

After her examination, Mrs. Kurtz removed three one-dollar bills from her purse and placed them on the doctor's desk.

"That's only three dollars," said the M.D. "My fee is ten!"

"They told me five!" said the woman sweetly.

* * *

CONSULTATION
A medical term meaning "share the wealth"

* * *

Doctor Kaplan approached his eighty-three-year-old patient in the hospital room. "Mr. Adler, you're the best patient we've ever had in this hospital, and because you've been so cooperative I'm going to tell you something we don't usually tell a patient. I'm sorry—but you're going to die. Is there anyone you'd like to see?"

"Yes," answered Adler. "I'd like to see another doctor!"

* * *

Stein, aged sixty-five, visited the office of his son, Dr. Stein, and asked for something that would increase his sexual potency. The M.D. gave his father a shot and then refused to accept a fee. Nevertheless, Stein insisted on giving him ten dollars.

A week later, Stein was back for another injection, and this time handed his son twenty dollars.

"But Pop! Shots are only ten dollars!"

"Take it!" said Stein. "The extra ten is from Mama!"

* * *

On his seventy-fifth birthday, Turtletaub rushed into a physician's office. "Doctor," he exclaimed, "I've got a date tonight with a twenty-two-year-old girl . . . you gotta give me something to pep me up!"

The M.D. smiled sympathetically and supplied the old man with a prescription. Later that night, out of curiosity, the medical man phoned his elderly patient. "Did the medicine help?"

"It's wonderful!" replied Turtletaub. "Seven times already!"

"That's great!" agreed the doctor. "And what about the girl?"

"The girl?" said Turtletaub. "She didn't get here yet!"

"Is your nephew Irving a good doctor?"

"Good? He's such a lovely boy, last year I needed an operation and I couldn't afford it. So he touched up the X-rays!"

* * *

"My son-in-law, the doctor, has been treating a patient for yellow jaundice for twenty years! He just found out the man was Chinese."

"Ain't that somethin'?"

"What's terrible is—he cured him!"

* * *

After examining Bloomberg, the doctor said, "You're going to need quite a bit of treatment. The fee will be a hundred dollars."

"Doctor, I'm a poor man," pleaded Bloomberg. "Give me a break!"

"All right," said the physician, "make it fifty dollars."

"Times are bad, Doctor, and I have three children to support!"

"Okay—twenty-five dollars!"

"I only work three days a week—couldn't you make it a little less?"

"Make it ten dollars!" said the frustrated physician. "But why do you come to me? I'm a specialist. You know I'm expensive!"

"When it comes to my health," said Bloomberg, "money is no object!"

Sid Berk, California's Vogue Shoes prez, broke up pals at the health club with this one:

A man sat before Dr. Gluckstein, the aged but renowned urinary-disorders specialist.

"My trouble," complained the man, "is that I can't pee!"

"How old are you?" asked Dr. Gluckstein.

"I'm ninety-three!"

"It's all right," said the famous urologist. "You peed enough!"

* * *

"Doctor, my feet hurt so bad—when I leave here, what should I do?"

"Take a taxi!" advised the podiatrist.

* * *

PSYCHIATRIST
A Jewish doctor who hates the sight of blood

* * *

"I got good news and bad news about our son," said Mrs. Smuckler to her husband.

"Give me the bad news first!" said Mr. Smuckler.

"Our boy's become a homosexual!"

"And what's the good news?"

"He's going with a rich doctor!"

Feldman, seated at the same table in a restaurant with Lerner, noticed that the poor man had nothing but gums to chew with. Feldman pulled some false teeth out of his pocket and offered them to his dinner companion. They were too loose.

Feldman volunteered another set of dentures. This time they were too tight. The next set, however, fit perfectly.

"Thanks very much!" said Lerner. "What a pleasure to sit at the same table with such a fine dentist!"

"Whatta ya talkin', dentist!" said Feldman. "I'm an *undertaker!*"

* * *

Steinberg felt a cold coming on, so he went to a doctor. Before Steinberg could explain his ailment, the nurse sent him into the next room and told him to strip. A man was standing there with his clothes under one arm and a package under the other.

"Can you imagine," complained Steinberg to his companion, "that nurse sent me in here to take off all my clothes—I only got a sore throat!"

"That's nothing!" said the man. "I came here to deliver a package!"

* * *

Doctor: All right, what seems to be the trouble?

Pincus: You went to school for ten years ... you tell me!

* * *

"Mrs. Sussman," said the psychiatrist, "there's nothing physically wrong with your little boy. But I'm afraid he does have an Oedipus complex!"

"Oedipus, shmedipus!" retorted Mrs. Sussman. "Just so long as he loves his mother!"

* * *

LOX
A herring with high blood pressure

* * *

Mrs. Garfunkel needed an intimate examination and decided that instead of going to a regular doctor she would patronize her son's friend, a gynecologist. Besides, since the boy had grown up in the neighborhood, she felt more comfortable about him.

Once Mrs. Garfunkel was on the examination table, the doctor, wearing rubber gloves, inspected and probed the woman's most private parts.

When he finished, Mrs. Garfunkel said, "Sammy, your mama knows you're making a living like this?"

Vaudevillians Smith and Dale were famous for their doctor sketch. This is a tiny chunk:

Dale: What are your fees, Doctor?

Smith: I charge ten dollars the first visit and five dollars for the second visit.

Dale: Well, Doctor, it's nice to see you again! What should I do?

Smith: Take the same medicine I gave you last time!

* * *

Mrs. Weinberg, age eighty-six, walked into a doctor's office to be examined.

"What's your complaint?" asked the M.D.

"I feel tired and run-down!" she said.

"I'm sorry," said the physician, "but I can't make you any younger!"

"All I want you should do," said Mrs. Weinberg, "is make me older!"

* * *

"Stop shaking your arms and making those pained faces at me," said Dr. Braverman, the dentist. "I haven't even started drilling yet!"

"I know that!" exclaimed Mrs. Kutcher, pulling the cotton out of her mouth to speak. "But you're standing on my corns!"

Doctor: The check you gave me came back!

Krinsky: So did my arthritis.

* * *

Comedian Buddy Lester heard a fellow seeking advice from a doctor at a cocktail party. "Hey, Doc," asked the man, "how do you stop a Jewish girl from screwing?"

"Marry her!"

* * *

Overheard at the same cocktail party:

"Morris, I want you to meet Doctor Sussman! Don't stand up, he's only a dentist!"

* * *

Dr. Vogel, the dentist, finished his examination on a pretty young patient. "Miss Bassman," he said, "I'm afraid I'm going to have to pull out your wisdom teeth!"

"Oh, my!" exclaimed the girl. "I'd rather have a baby!"

"Well," said Dr. Vogel, "could you make up your mind so I can adjust the chair?"

Dr. Ramon Spritzler, Beverly Hills internist, relaxes patients with this beaut:

Klein, eighty-seven, married a twenty-one-year-old girl. After their honeymoon, he went to a doctor. "She's only a young girl," said Klein. "I want to keep her satisfied. What should I do?"

"My advice," said the physician, "is that you should take in a boarder!"

One year later, Klein revisited the medical man. "How's your wife?" asked the doctor.

"She's pregnant!" said the old man proudly.

"And how's the boarder?"

"She's pregnant, too!"

* * *

SHABBES

"Rabbi Jacobs, I need fifty dollars to get out of debt," sobbed Gottlieb. "I keep praying to God for help but He doesn't send it!"

"Don't lose faith," said the rabbi. "Keep praying."

After Gottlieb left his house, the rabbi felt sorry for him. "I don't make much money," he thought, "but that poor man needs it. I'll give him twenty-five dollars out of my own pocket."

A week later, the rabbi stopped Gottlieb and said, "Here, God sent this to you!"

Back in his home, Gottlieb bowed his head. "Thank you, Lord!" he said. "But next time you send money, don't send it through Rabbi Jacobs—that crook kept half of it!"

Siegel and Posner, complete strangers, were sitting across from each other, nude, in the steam room. "I never met you before," said Siegel, "and yet I'll bet you were born in Brooklyn!"

"That's right!" said Posner.

"In fact," said Siegel to his naked companion, "you're from my old neighborhood, Bensonhurst, and you went to the Seventy-ninth Street Synagogue, and your rabbi was Nathan Nussbaum!"

"Amazing!" said Posner. "You can tell all that just by looking at me?"

"Of course," said Siegel. "Rabbi Nussbaum always did cut on the bias!"

* * *

"I'm so upset," said Hershberg to a rabbi. "I took my son-in-law into my clothing business and yesterday I caught him kissing one of the models!"

"Have a little patience!" advised the rabbi. "After all, guys will be guys. So he kissed one of the models, it's not so terrible."

"But you don't understand," said Hershberg. "I make *men's* clothes!"

* * *

The sexton ran into the rabbi's office and exclaimed excitedly, "Rabbi, I have terrible news to report! Burglars must've broken in last night—they stole ninety thousand dollars' worth of pledges!"

* * *

Two rabbis were having lunch. "Some of my congregation is switching over to the Quakers!" complained the first.

"Is that a fact?" said the second.

"Yes, some of my best Jews are Friends!"

* * *

Scientists concluded that the icecap was going to melt and the whole world would be flooded within six months. When the news broke, religious leaders went into deep conference.

The Protestant hierarchy released a statement: "Because of the impending disaster Protestants will go to church and pray for two hours every day."

Then the Catholics made an announcement: "Because of the coming deluge, Catholics will make every other day—all day—a day of prayer for the next six months!"

Rabbis from all over the land convened, then they too issued a message to the world: "Because the whole world will be flooded in six months, Jews will learn how to live underwater!"

I heard Alan King tell this gem:

A little boy came home from Sunday School, and his father said, "What did the rabbi teach you today?"

"Well," said the youngster, "two thousand years ago the Jews wanted to escape from the bad Egyptians, so Moses had the Jews build this suspension bridge across the Red Sea. Then they loaded it down with dynamite. The Jews escaped across the bridge, and when all the Egyptians chased them, they blew up the bridge and all the Egyptians were drowned."

"Is that what the rabbi told you?" asked the surprised father.

"No," said the boy, "but you'd never believe the crazy story he *did* tell us!"

"How come you decided to become a Jew?"

"Well, I used to be an atheist, but I gave it up!"

"Why?"

"No holidays!"

* * *

Everything in Southern California is a little far out—even religion. There's a Reform temple in Beverly Hills that's so Reform that on the holiest of days—Yom Kippur—they have a sign on the door saying "Closed for the Jewish Holidays."

* * *

Samuels met Bloomfeld at the race track. "How is it," asked Samuels, "you win all the time and I always lose?"

"Because," boasted Bloomfeld, "before I come to the track on Saturday afternoon I go to the temple and I pray."

Samuels decided to follow his friend's example. The following Saturday they met again, but Samuels was still a loser. "I don't understand it," he complained. "I went to the temple this morning and I lost every race!"

"What temple did you go to?" asked Bloomfeld.

"Beth Israel!"

"You idiot!" cried Bloomfeld. "That's for trotters!"

* * *

Monty Hall, America's beloved TV host of "Let's Make a Deal," is also one of Hollywood's biggest fund-raisers. Here is a story he tells at charity dinners:

Shimkin had been shipwrecked for twenty years on a desert island when finally he was rescued by a passing ship.

"What did you do to keep busy all those years?" asked the captain of the rescue vessel.

"I went into the building business!" replied Shimkin. Whereupon he took the captain to a corner of the island and showed him a beautiful synagogue.

"That's incredible!" said the sailing master.

"That's nothin'," said Shimkin. This time he led him to the opposite end of the island and displayed another magnificently constructed house of worship.

"I don't understand," said the captain. "You're the only person on the island—why did you need two synagogues?"

"This one I belong to," explained Shimkin, "but the other one—I wouldn't set foot inside if they paid me!"

Some Jewish boys don't have the same attitude toward religion as their fathers. Eisenstein sent a telegram to his son: DON'T FORGET YOM KIPPUR STARTS TOMORROW.

The boy sent a wire back: PUT $100 ON THE NOSE FOR ME.

* * *

Schlossberg was a very religious man. While visiting a cousin in St. Louis, he said to him, "Our rabbi is so holy that he talks to God."

"Talks with God?" said his relative. "How do you know that?"

"He told us so himself!" replied Schlossberg.

"But maybe he lied!"

"Dumbbell! Would a man who talks to God tell lies?"

* * *

The rabbi had stood before the synagogue's board of directors for almost an hour pleading with them to buy a chandelier for the temple.

When he'd finished, Blum, the elderly president, stood up. "What're we wasting time talkin'?" he demanded. "First of all, a chandelier—we ain't got nobody could even *spell* it!

"Second, we ain't got nobody here who could *play* it!

"And third, what we need in the synagogue is more *light!*"

*   *   *

Jacobson, aged ninety, had lived through beatings in Polish pogroms, concentration camps in Germany, and dozens of other anti-Semitic experiences.

"Oh, Lord!" he prayed, sitting in synagogue. "Isn't it true that we are your chosen people?"

And from the heavens boomed a voice: "Yes, Jacobson, the Jews are my chosen people!"

"Well, then," wailed the old man, "isn't it time you chose somebody else?"

*   *   *

Rabbi Birnbaum sat in temple all alone, tears streaming down his cheeks. He just learned that his only son had deserted the faith of his forefathers and had become a Protestant.

The rabbi was sobbing uncontrollably when suddenly he heard the voice of God: "What is troubling you?"

"I'm so ashamed," cried the Rabbi. "My only son gave up being a Jew and became a Christian!"

"*Yours* too?" replied the Lord.

Monahan stopped his friend Weinberg and said, "Say, I've always been meanin' to ask you a question!"

"You could ask me anything!" said Weinberg.

"What is a *bris?*"

"My friend," said Weinberg, "you know the expression 'you can't take it with you'?"

"Yeah!"

"A *bris* means you can't even keep it all while you're here!"

*   *   *

Ben Hakim, the Honolulu huckster of precious gems, tells about Rabbi Resnick and Father Foley, seated next to each other on a jet to Chicago. "Say, Father," said the rabbi, "have you ever been out with a woman?"

"Of course not!" exclaimed the shocked priest. "That would be like your eating ham!"

"I'll tell you something," said the rabbi. "I've tried both and believe me, there's no comparison!"

*   *   *

Kramer and Grosberg were Orthodox and even wore beards, black hats, and long black coats. They passed a Catholic church, peeked inside, and noticed a service in progress. Friends and relatives had

110

crowded together in the pews to witness a group of nuns taking their vows.

"Those girls," explained Kramer, "are becoming the brides of Christ!"

"Let's go in and take a look!" said Grosberg.

The moment they sat down to watch the marriage ceremony, an usher walked up to them. "What are you two doing here?"

"It's all right," said Kramer. "We're from the groom's side!"

* * *

Father Duffy and Rabbi Muchnik were chatting at a town meeting. "Could I ask you a question?" inquired Father Duffy.

"Of course," said Rabbi Muchnik.

"It's always been my understanding that the Apostles were Jews. Isn't that correct?"

"Absolutely right!" replied the rabbi.

"Then how the deuce did the Jews let go of a good thing like the Catholic Church and let the Eye-talians grab it?"

* * *

Father Clanahan and Father McNurty were concluding a theological discussion. As they parted, Father Clanahan said, "By the way, what are you giving up for Lent?"

"Matzoh-ball soup!" replied the other priest.

111

McLain dialed the number of a large law firm. When the switchboard operator answered, he asked, "Is Mr. Berkowitz in?"

"No, he's not," she said. "This is Yom Kippur."

"Well," said McLain, "when do you expect him, Miss Kippur?"

* * *

Father Shannon and Rabbi Rudnick were sitting ringside at the prizefights. Just before the main event, one of the fighters knelt in his corner and crossed himself.

"Tell me," said the rabbi, "does that help?"

"Not a bit if he can't fight!" answered the priest.

* * *

Shulman had been given the job of repainting the town's Catholic church. After a week, the Mother Superior called him into her office.

"Mr. Shulman, we're very pleased with your work," she said, "but there are some things you must stop doing if you are to continue here!"

"Yes?" said Shulman.

"First," said the Mother Superior, "remove your hat when you come into the church. Second, don't wash your hands in the holy water. And third, stop calling me Mother *Shapiro!*"

*   *   *

Young Sammy was playing with little Timothy in the street. Suddenly, Timothy exclaimed: "My priest knows more than your rabbi!"

"Why shouldn't he?" said Sammy. "You tell him everything!"

*   *   *

Robert Briscoe, the Jewish former lord mayor of Dublin, had the typical Irish charm and wit. He once said that after he was elected, out of deference to him, they called leprechauns "lepre*cohens.*"

At a fund-raising affair in New York, Briscoe told the audience that most of the four thousand Jews in Ireland were Orthodox. Recently, however, a Reform synagogue had been built in Dublin.

"As you know," he said, "Ireland's population is ninety-five percent Catholic, and foreigners on sightseeing trips often ask what the new building is. Cabdrivers have been known to answer, 'Oh, that's the new Protestant synagogue!' "

Sam Young, West Coast Manager of *Amusement Business Magazine*, made this contribution:

Rabbi Grossman and Father O'Malley were seated beside each other at a banquet. "Have some ham," offered the priest.

"I'm afraid not," answered the rabbi.

"C'mon, try some," the priest encouraged. "It's real good!"

"Thanks, but I don't eat that kind of meat because of my religion."

"It's really delicious!" said Father O'Malley five minutes later. "You oughta try this ham, you'd like it!"

"No thank you!" replied Rabbi Grossman.

After dinner, the two men shook hands. "Tell me," said the Jewish clergyman, "do you enjoy sex with your wife?"

"Oh, Rabbi, you should know I'm not allowed to be married," said the priest. "I can't have sex!"

"You ought to try it," said the rabbi. "It's better than ham!"

*　　*　　*

Abie wanted to marry his Irish Rose, and they stood in the temple office. "I'd be very happy to officiate," said the rabbi, "but I'd like to be assured that Rose has a little Jew in her!"

"Oh, I do!" the bride-to-be exclaimed. "Abie couldn't wait!"

The Jews and the Irish have traditionally stood side by side in the bonds of good fellowship. So much so, that should there ever be a Jewish-Catholic prayer, it would begin:

"Oy vay, Maria!"

* * *

THE END . . .

of the Jewish jokes, that is. Please turn the book and start again, to read the Irish jokes. (Unless you're Jewish, of course, in which case you should read this section again—only this time read it without lamenting the cost of the book.)

NOTE

If you are Jewish and find it difficult to laugh at yourself or if you have become angry, there is one way to have a laugh and lessen your anger. Follow these instructions carefully:

(1) Every time you see the word *Jewish* (or any slang with the same meaning), substitute one of the following words:

> Polish, Italian, Chinese, German, British, Icelandic, Brazilian, Canadian, Filipino, Hungarian, Egyptian, Russian, Australian, Norwegian, African, Korean, Gypsy, Afghanistanian, etc. See how easy it is to be funny!

(2) Now you can read the Irish jokes . . . and by the way, we've already done a book on Polish and Italian jokes, in case you'd appreciate a laugh at *their* expense.

MAZEL TOV!

(an unpaid political announcement)

ADVANCE CRITICAL PRAISE!

Praise the Lord! Saint Patty himself would skip an uptown wake to read this blessed book. It's so funny that even you shanty types can get the jokes. Sure an' I roared at every joke, and everyone at Fitzpatrick's joined in, even Father O'Hennessy.

It was so good I was able to read the part about those Hebrew folks in a little less than a week, and I realized that the reason why they never feel good is that they just don't know how to drink. All you hear is eat, eat, eat!

Anyway, get a copy of the book and pass it around your local parish. It ought to be good for a few laughs at the pub, too. Just be careful if you read the jokes out loud . . . I'm still nursing a shiner from last week's brawl at the steamfitters' and firefighters' picnic.

> Sean O'Hara, Editor
> *The South Boston Shamrock News*

THE OFFICIAL JEWISH/IRISH JOKE BOOK

by
Larry Wilde

Illustrations by Ron Wing

PINNACLE BOOKS • **NEW YORK CITY**

THE OFFICIAL IRISH JOKE BOOK

INTRODUCTION 1

1. SHILLELAGHS 5
   Brawling ... Cops ... Maids ... Limericks ... Married Life ... Wakes

2. SHAMROCKS 31
   Double meanings

3. SHEBANG 39
   Bartenders ... Drinking ... Drunks ... Toasts ... Saloons ... St. Patrick's Day

4. SHENANIGANS 69
   Immigrants ... Ireland ... England ... Old Age ... Police ... Politics

5. SAINTS 97
   Church ... Confession ... Nuns ... Sins ... Sex ... Religion ... Rabbis

INTRODUCTION

Pat: What would you be if you
weren't Irish?
Mike: I'd be ashamed!

There are approximately 16,000,000 people of Irish descent living in America and
every last one of them is vehemently proud
of that heritage.

Surely other ethnic groups feel strongly
about where they or their ancestors were
born; it is just that the Sons of Erin seem
to make a bigger fuss over their Hibernian
heritage than other groups do over their
respective origins.

That fierce pride can best be seen in this
pointed exchange:

If I wasn't Irish, know what I'd
rather be?
What?
Dead!

1

As a boy, I remember anxiously awaiting our next-door neighbor Timothy Boyle to come sauntering up the street. His arrival meant a peppermint Life Saver. It was a daily treat, for besides having the candy, Mister Boyle always had a twinkle in his eye, a smile on his lips, and Old Grand-Dad on his breath.

Years later, I finally figured out why he always carried the peppermints.

The truth of it was that kindly Mister Boyle was a secret drinker. His family never knew he drank, until one night he came home sober—and the dog bit him.

To me, Timothy Boyle has always typified the blessed followers of St. Patrick. Though a day never passed that Timothy didn't enjoy a brew or two, there were so many other winning traits to his spirited personality that I couldn't help but love him. With his brogue and grin and lively step, he led me to believe that Ireland was the greatest place on earth.

Mister Boyle was overly sentimental. His emotions ran from the deepest sorrow to the wildest joy. He had a great reverence for the Catholic Church. And his love of the mother country bordered on blind adoration.

Through him, I learned that an Irishman loves a good brawl, the food and drink at a wake, and the sweet tones of a lyric tenor. At times, Mister Boyle became volatile, vindictive, and surly, often taking insult at the slightest provocation.

But deep in that angelic soul lived the love of laughter. Timothy Boyle never passed me a peppermint without passing on the latest gag. And with it a laugh that shook the very beer inside his beloved, bloated belly.

Though he constantly cracked quips and spoke funny sayings—these are the words I remember him by most:

Me boy, there are only two kinds of people in the world. Those who are Irish! And those who wish they were!

Timothy Boyle would have loved the jokes you are about to read. I hope you do too!

LARRY WILDE
Hollywood, California

June, 1974

SHILLELAGHS

How does a newspaper story about an
Irish social event begin?
"Among the injured were . . ."

*   *   *

A dentist, young Doctor Malone
Got a charming girl patient alone;
  And in his depravity,
  He filled the wrong cavity—
And my how his practice has grown.

*   *   *

"Is O'Brien's wife tough?"
"Tough? Say, she could knit barbed
wire with two crowbars!"

Jim Belcher, head of Chilton TV Productions, kills dinner guests with this one:

Haggarty ran a red light and plowed headlong into a car driven by Father Cogan. The auto turned over three times and the priest, thrown from the vehicle, lay stunned beside the road.

Haggarty rushed over and said, "I'm terribly sorry, Father!"

"Saints above!" said the shaken priest. "You almost killed me!"

"Here," said Haggarty, "I've got a little sacramental Jack Daniels. Take some and you'll feel a lot better!"

Father Cogan took a couple of large swigs and continued his tirade. "What were you thinkin' about, man? You nearly launched me into eternity!"

"I'm sorry, Father," said Haggarty. "Take a few more sips, it'll ease your nerves."

After the priest had almost finished the entire bottle, he said, "Why don't you have a drink?"

"No thanks, your Reverence," said Haggarty, "I'll just sit here and wait for the police!"

Rosaleen, the Irish maid, had been entertaining her sailor boyfriend. Mrs. Levin, her employer, wanting to be polite, asked, "And how long is his furlough?"

"Not as long as Mr. Levin's," said Rosaleen, blushing. "But it's thicker!"

*   *   *

McClain arrived home with two black eyes, a swollen ear, and a mashed nose. "What happened?" asked his wife.

"I had a bit of an argument with that little German fella, Schotts," explained McClain. "He said the Irish weren't the only handsome and intelligent men in the world. So I gives him the back of me hand in the front of his puss and a beautiful fight we had!"

"How could you be lettin' a little sawed-off shrimp of a man," shouted Mrs. McClain, "a runt, a mere midget, a droolin' dwarf talk to—"

"Hush now," interrupted McClain. "Don't be speakin' disrepectful of the dead!"

*   *   *

Don Sutton, the great Los Angeles Dodgers pitcher, also has a great sense of humor. Here's one he tells on the winter banquet circuit:

At a lunch break Costigan started talk-

ing to Clark, who was a Protestant. "Do you know the difference," asked Costigan, "between a baseball game and a Protestant Sunday School?"

"Tell me," said Clark.

"At a Protestant Sunday School they sing 'Stand Up For Jesus,' and at a baseball game they holler, 'Sit down, for Christ's sake!'"

*   *   *

Mrs. Cochrane was standing beside the coffin of her dead husband. Their son stood at her elbow. The mourners, one by one, passed in review.

"He's feelin' no pain now," said Mrs. Croy. "What did he die of?"

"Poor fella," said Mrs. Cochrane. "He died of the gonorrhea."

Another woman gazed at the corpse. "He's well out of it now," she said. "He's got a smile of serenity on his face. What did he die from?"

"He died of the gonorrhea!" said the widow.

Suddenly, the son pulled his mother aside. "Mom," he said, "that's a terrible thing to say about Pop. He didn't die of gonorrhea. He died of diarrhea!"

"I know that," said Mrs. Cochrane, "but I'd rather have them thinkin' he died like a sport—instead of the shit that he was!"

"Won't you sit down, Miss?" said a man on the subway to an attractive Irish lass. "No thank you! I'm in a terrible hurry!"

* * *

Mrs. McDermot, eight months' pregnant, stood in the crowd enjoying the St. Patrick's Day parade. People kept pushing and shoving, not noticing her delicate condition. Finally, Riley the cop said to her, "Missus, why don't you go on home. The little fella can't see anyway!"

"I know," said Mrs. McDermot, "but I left me drawers at home, so at least, he can hear the music!"

* * *

Last St. Patrick's Day, a New York department store ran the following ad in the papers:

> Bagels,
> Begorrah!
> (Green ones, yet)
Lox and cream cheese . . . tenth floor.

* * *

Cruise Director Tony Craig gets screams with this one aboard the *Leonardo da Vinci:*

10

Higgins lived in Staten Island, New York, and worked in Manhattan. He had to take the ferryboat home every night. One evening, he got down to the ferry and found there was a wait for the next boat. So he decided to stop at a nearby bar. Before long, Higgins was feeling no pain.

When he got back to the ferry slip, the ferryboat was just eight feet from the dock. Higgins, afraid of missing this one and being late for dinner, took a running leap and landed right on the deck of the boat.

"How did you like that jump, buddy?" said Higgins to a deck hand.

"It was great," said the sailor. "But why didn't you wait? We were just pulling in!"

* * *

Did you hear about the Irish psychiatrist who used a Murphy bed instead of a couch?

* * *

Comedian Jack Denton relates this true incident:

"I was eating at the Blarney Castle one evening when the Irish waitress spilled the soup all over my jacket."

" 'Ah!' " she exclaimed. 'And aren't you a fine broth of a lad!' "

11

A rich Texan sitting in a Dublin pub began talking to Kernan. "Ireland isn't a bad country," said the man from the Lone Star State, "but it doesn't compare to Texas!"

"An' why not?" asked Kernan.

"In Texas a man can get on a train early Monday morning, have his breakfast, his lunch, his supper, and then go to sleep. When he gets up Tuesday morning, he's still on the same train, and he can have his breakfast, his lunch, his supper, and go to bed again. And do you know that when he gets up Wednesday morning and gets off that train, he's still in Texas?"

"What's so unusual about that?" said Kernan. "We have slow trains in Ireland too!"

IRISH DIAMOND
A *sham rock*

* * *

Cudahy, grogged to the gills, stood watching the St. Patrick's Day parade. Unconsciously, he dropped his lit cigarette into an old mattress that was lying at the curb.

Just then the gray-haired members of the Ladies' Nursing Corps came strutting by. At the same time, the smoldering mattress began giving off a dreadful smell.

Cudahy sniffed a couple of times and bellowed to a nearby cop, "Officer, they're marchin' those nurses too fast!"

* * *

QUINLAN'S QUOTE
Noonan is sort of a politician's politician. If he's elected he's goin' to legalize graft.

* * *

Dugan listened to the Irish politician rant on and on about what was wrong with the government and why he should be elected.

After an hour, Dugan couldn't take much more. He stood up and said, "The trouble with you, me bucko, is that you have a diarrhea of words and a constipation of ideas!"

Keegan: Take a look at at this present I bought for Maggie. An emerald ring.

Fagan: This isn't an emerald. An emerald is green.

Keegan: Well, just wait'll she wears it awhile.

* * *

O'Leary worked for the Bethelem Steel Company for two years, but became so lazy his foreman wanted to fire him. The supervisor didn't have the heart to tell O'Leary to his face so he wrote him a letter.

At the end of the week, O'Leary showed up for work again. "Didn't you get my letter?" asked the foreman.

"Indeed I did, sir!"

"Did you read it?"

"I read it inside and outside."

"Then what are you doing here?"

"Inside, I read that I was fired," said O'Leary. "But on the outside it said, *'In five days return to Bethlehem Steel.'* So here I am!"

* * *

There was a young corporal of Kildare
Who was fondling a girl in a chair
    At the sixty-third stroke,
    The furniture broke
And his rifle went off in the air.

15

Clarence Pine, the Los Angeles Farmers Market enterpriser, returned from a vacation in Ireland and reported overhearing this conversation:

"Say, Reagan, heard you visited Dublin!"

"Indeed, I did!" said Reagan. "And a great city I found it to be. I was befriended by a lady who took me to her apartment, and then took off all her clothes. Why, I'll bet if I'd a played me cards right, I coulda kissed her!"

* * *

Quinn was sent by his employers, Carter Contracters, to the Giovanni funeral, since the dead man had been a member of the Carter construction gang. After the services, Quinn reported to his boss.

" 'Tis a curious custom, them Eyetalians have," said Quinn. "They put a twenty-dollar gold piece in the hand of the corpse before buryin' him."

"That's an old superstition," explained his boss. "It's to pay the man's way across the River Jordan."

"I hope that wop can swim," said Quinn. "I got the twenty in me pocket!"

* * *

Phyllis Kramer (husband Don is Les Brown's manager) tells friends she first heard her grandfather explain the difference between *blarney* and *baloney*:

16

Baloney is the unvarnished lie—laid on so thick you hate it.

Blarney is flattery—laid on so thin you love it.

To tell a woman who is forty she looks like sixteen is baloney. The blarney way of saying it is, "Tell me how old you are. I should like to know at what age women are most beautiful!"

* * *

O'Reilly lay dying when the pungent aroma of corned beef and cabbage being cooked by his wife brought a smile to his lips.

"Ah, darlin', let me leave this world a happy man," said O'Reilly. "Give me just a small bit of that stuff you're cookin'!"

"Sure an' I couldn't do that!" said Mrs. O'Reilly. "I'm savin' it for the wake!"

* * *

Healy had been cheating on his wife for years. One night, she finally confronted him with it. "So what?" Healey snarled.

"In fact," he went on, "I have a date tonight! And who do you think is gonna help me get dressed for my date? *You* are! And who do you think is gonna shine my shoes? *You* are! And do you know who's gonna tie my tie?"

"Yes," said Mrs. Healy. "The under-taker!"

17

At a stag party in back of Tamney's Tavern, Egan made a big hit with the boys when he gave the toast, *"To the happiest years of me life—spent between the legs of me wife!"*

Later, at home, Egan did not want to offend his wife, so he told her the toast was, *"Here's to the happiest moments of me life—spent in church beside me wife."*

The next day, a neighbor who had heard about the original toast from her own husband congratulated the unsuspected Mrs. Egan.

"It'd be grand if it were true," said Egan's wife. "But it's only happened twice. Once before we was married and once after. And the second time I had to wake him up after it was all over."

* * *

Molly had just arrived from the old country and immediately found work at the Perlmans as a maid. One day, to Mrs. Perlman's embarrassment, young Molly found something lying on the sheets while making up the bed.

In order to gloss over the matter lightly, her employer said, "Why, Molly, don't you use those things in Ireland?"

"Yes," said the girl, "but we don't skin them!"

Ralph Gallagher, Long Beach Elks Club entertainment director, heard this from an Elk:

Culkin opened the morning newspaper and was dumbfounded to read in the obituary column that he had died. He quickly phoned his best friend, Fennelly.

"Did you see the paper?" asked Culkin. "They say I died!"

"Yes, I saw it!" replied Fennelly. "Where are you callin' from?"

* * *

"That's a queer pair of stockings you have on, O'Delly—one's red and the other's green!"

"Yes," said O'Delly, "and I've got another pair at home just like it."

* * *

A famous Abbey Theatre thespian was lying on the psychiatrist's couch. The doctor asked, "Do you talk to your wife during intercourse?"

"Only if there's a telephone handy," replied the matinee idol.

* * *

"Your husband's a real he-man, ain't he?" asked Mrs. Cullen.

"Oh, yes," answered her friend. "He pulls out the stopper in the bathtub and then he battles the current!"

First woman: Did you hear about Mrs. Gaffney having quadruplets? I understand that only happens once every sixty thousand times.

Second woman: Glory be! When does she get her housework done?

McClannahan walked into the house after work one evening, and before he could take off his coat his wife lit into him. "Here I've been roasting over a hot stove," she shouted, "while you've been enjoying yourself passin' the day in that nice cool sewer!"

* * *

"Now that me mother's gone and left us," said Mrs. Gannon to her husband, "what sort of tombstone should we be gettin' for her—a plain one or something elaborate?"

"Somethin' good and *heavy*," replied Mr. Gannon.

* * *

"Is it true, O'Sullivan's lost a lot of weight?"

"I'll not be sayin' O'Sullivan's thin, but when he wears a red tie, he looks like a thermometer."

* * *

What's an Irish holiday?
Sitting on somebody else's stoop.

* * *

Mrs. McMahon went berserk one afternoon. She broke every dish and cup and

reduced her usually spotless kitchen to shambles. The police arrived and took her to the city's mental institution.

The head psychiatrist sent for her husband.

"Do you know any reason," asked the shrink, "why your wife should suddenly lose her mind?"

"I'm just as surprised as you are," answered Mr. McMahon. "I can't imagine what got into her. She's always been such a quiet, hard-working woman. Why, she hasn't been out of the kitchen in twenty years!"

* * *

Fogarty, arrested for murder, bribed Hennessy on the jury to oppose the death penalty and hold out for a manslaughter charge.

The jury was out a long time, and finally came in with a verdict of manslaughter. Fogarty rushed up to Hennessy and whispered, "I'm tremendously obliged. Did you have a hard time of it?"

"Terrible!" said Hennessy. "The other eleven all wanted to acquit you!"

* * *

What's dumber than a dumb Irishman?" A smart Scot.

"Hey there!" an irate passerby shouted up to a group of bricklayers two stories from the ground. The workmen looked down curiously.

"One of you just dropped a brick, and it came within an inch of hitting me on the head."

"Don't trouble to return it," shouted Moriarty, the foreman. "We've got plenty more of 'em up here!"

* * *

Bill Bell, prez of Bell Sound Studios in Hollywood came up with this lulu:

McElwain, the father of twelve children, went to visit Mrs. McElwain in the hospital. She had just given birth to Number Thirteen.

Waiting to congratulate his wife, McElwain tiptoed up to her bed and kissed her gently on the cheek. Half asleep, she smiled and chided him, "Oh, Mac, startin' in again, are ya?"

* * *

Mr. and Mrs. Connell were in the midst of another one of their domestic battles. "The trouble around here is that there's no harmony!" said Mrs. Connell.

"Them's my sentiments exactly!" agreed Mr. Connell.

He led Mrs. Connell to their apartment window and pointed. "See those two horses out there pullin' that load of scrap up the

hill," said Mr. Connell. "That's the way we should be—pullin' together like a pair of horses along the road of life."

"How can we now," said Mrs. Connell, "when one of us is a jackass!"

* * *

"Good morning," said the doctor to Mrs. Couglin. "Did you take your husband's temperature, like I told you?"

"Yes, I did, Doctor," said Mrs. Couglin. "I borrowed a barometer and placed it in his chest. It said *Very Dry*, so I brought him a pint of beer an' he's gone back to work!"

* * *

St. Patrick chased the snakes out of Ireland. Now, if someone'll only chase the baboons out of Congress.

* * *

Ron Carver, television writer and UCLA comedy lecturer, offered this plum to warm the cockles of an Irish heart:

"What would you be chargin' me for a funeral notice in your paper?" inquired Dempsey.

"Fifty cents per inch!" replied the editor.

"Good heavens! An' me poor brother was six feet high!"

One summer evening in New York a pretty Irish girl was walking across Broadway and was struck by a truck. She flew into the air, and by the time her body settled on the street all of her clothes had been stripped away.

A passing priest saw the accident. As a crowd began to gather, he rushed over to the naked, unconscious girl, removed his hat and placed it over the junction where her legs were joined together.

McMannus heard the commotion, staggered out of a saloon, forced his way through the onlookers and stood beside the priest. He stared down at the nude girl and the hat that had been placed over her crotch.

"Saints preserve us," he exclaimed to the priest. "First thing we've got to do is get that man out of there!"

Private O'Grady, on sentry duty, had orders to allow no one to smoke near his post. A lieutenant with a lighted cigar was passing by, and O'Grady ordered him to put it out at once.

The officer, with a gesture of disgust, threw away his stogie. No sooner was his back turned than the private picked it up and disappeared into the sentry box.

The lieutenant happened to look around and saw smoke coming from the sentry box. "Hey," he shouted, "you're not supposed to smoke on guard duty!"

"Smoking, sir?" said O'Grady, "I'm only keeping it lit to show the corporal of the guard, when he comes, as evidence against you!"

* * *

A traveler, passing through a small town, saw an elaborate funeral going down Main Street. He stopped McGuire to ask him about it.

"Who died?" inquired the stranger.

"I can't say for sure," answered McGuire, "but I think it's the one in the hearse."

* * *

What's an Irish chauffeur-driven limousine called?

The paddy wagon.

If your son flunks out of school, is illiterate, and antisocial, what can he grow up to be?

An Irish cop!

* * *

There was a young couple named Kelly
Who were forced to walk belly to belly,
  Because in their haste
  They used library paste
Which they thought was vaginal jelly.

* * *

At an airlines reservation desk, a man wearing a cowboy hat said to the clerk, "My name is Brown. Spelled B-r-o-w-n. I'm from Texas! I'm six feet tall. I'm white from the top of my head to the tip of my toes. And I hate the Irish!"

On the plane, the Texan sat down, turned to the man beside him, and said, "Howdy. Name's Brown. Spelled B-r-o-w-n. I'm from Texas. I'm six feet tall. I'm white from the top of my head to the tip of my toes. And I hate micks!"

"How do you do?" said the man. "My name is Patrick Michael Walsh. I'm from Dublin. I'm five feet six inches tall. I'm white from the top of me head to the tip of me toes—except for me rectum which is brown. Spelled B-r-o-w-n."

SHAMROCKS

The Irish are famous for uttering remarks that contradict each other. These statements of paradox—although appearing to have two opposite meanings—may nontheless have a logic of their own. For instance:

O'Shay had been having a bitter argument with a friend, and now he was about to finish him off once and for all.

"The sooner I never see your face again," said O'Shay, "the better it will be for both of us when we meet!"

Then there was the great Irish lover who said, "Darlin, 'tis a great comfort to be alone, especially when your sweetheart is with you!"

Milligan and Flynn were discussing architecture. "Modern buildings are more beautiful than the old ones!" declared Milligan.

"An' will you show me," insisted Flynn, "any modern building that has lasted as long as the ancient ones!"

"Do you know McKeown?
"Indeed, I know him well."
"Can a person believe what he says?"
"Yes and no. I've found out that if he tells you the truth, you can believe every word of it—but when he lies, you'd better have no confidence in him at all."

* * *

"The sun is all very well," said McGrath, "but the moon is worth two of it!"
"How's that?" asked Buckley.
"Well, the moon gives us light in the nighttime when we *want it*, whereas the sun's with us in the daytime, when we don't have any *occasion for it!*"

* * *

"Begorrah, I'd give me life savin's to know where I was goin' to die," said Mrs. McCall.
"And what good," asked her neighbor, "would it do you if you knew!"
"Plenty," said Mrs. McCall. "I'd stay away from that place."

* * *

"After all," said McQuinlan, " 'tis a great pleasure to be missed by someone."
"Sure it is," said his pal, "if you can be there to enjoy it!"

32

"If Mr. Smith comes back before I return," said the manager to a clerk, "tell him that I will meet him at two o'clock!"

"Yes, sorr!" said Miss Bryant. "But what shall I tell him if he doesn't come?"

* * *

"If they ever drop the bomb on us," said Mrs. Hogarty, "they'll blow us all to maternity!"

"Yeah," said Mrs. Shea, "and we won't know who to blame, either!"

* * *

"If one of us gets there late, and the other isn't there," asked McHatton, "how will he know if the other one has been there and gone, or if he didn't come yet?"

"We'll easily fix that," said Riordan. "If I get there first, I'll make a chalk mark on the sidewalk, and if you get there first, you'll rub it out."

* * *

Hugh Baker, the talented serigraph artist, came up with this poignantly drawn picture of Irish life:

"Tell me, O'Callaghan," asked the priest, "would you like yourself to be buried in a Protestant graveyard?"

"Not me, Father," replied O'Callaghan, "I'd rather die first!"

McGuffy read a newspaper ad in the Help Wanted section. He quickly wrote the following note:

"Gentlemen, I noticed your advertisement for an organist and music teacher, either lady or gentlemen. Having been both for many years, I offer you my services."

* * *

"What's a pessimist?" asked O'Day.

"He's a feller," said Coyle, "what burns his bridges behind him an' then crosses them before he comes to them."

* * *

"Abstinence," said Father Cleary. "is a wonderful thing, Bragan!"

"Sure and it is, Father," said Bragan, "if practiced in moderation."

* * *

Mrs. McMilligan and Mrs. Conway were coming back from church. "Me son Jimmy's comin' home tomorra!" said Mrs. McMilligan.

"That's nice!" retorted Mrs. Conway. "But I thought he was sent up fer five years!"

"He was that!" answered her companion, "But the lad got time off fer good behavior!"

"Oh, my!" exclaimed Mrs. Conway. "It must be a blessin' to you, to know you've got such a fine son!"

* * *

McCarthy and O'Toole met on the street and rushed up to shake hands. As they did, both men realized they didn't know each other.

"Beggin' your pardon," asked McCarthy.

"Faith, I thought it was you, and you thought it was me," said O'Toole, "and bejabbers, it wasn't neither of us!"

* * *

"Young man," said the judge, looking sternly at the defendant. "It's alcohol and alcohol alone that's responsible for your present sorry state!"

"I'm glad to hear you say that," replied Mooney, with a sigh of relief. "Everybody else says it's all my fault!"

* * *

"I'm going to the race track today," announced Garrigan.

"Good luck, to ya!" said his friend.

"I just hope I break even," said Garrigan. "I need the money!"

"How many fathoms?" shouted Captain McLain to a sailor on the deck below who was holding the anchor chain.

"Can't touch bottom, sir!" said the sailor.

"Well, damn it," cried the captain. "how near the bottom do you come?

* * *

Gilhooley fell out of the window and crashed to his death. Mrs. Gilhooley collected the insurance, as well as the federal, state, and Social Security benefits. But then came the lawyers, relatives, government deductions, bills, inheritance tax, etc.

When the doctor came to see her, she was in an awful state. "Sometimes," cried the widow, "I almost wish me husband hadn't fallen out of the window!"

* * *

O'Leery: I couldn't pay me three-dollar fine so I had to go to jail for six days.

McKay: An' how much did you spend to get drunk?

O'Leery: Oh, about three dollars

McKay: Three dollars? You damn fool, if you hadn't spent your three dollars for whiskey, you'd a had your three dollars for your fine.

36

Gaby Rivera gets screams from his Palm Springs guests with this one:

Mrs. O'Rourke and Mrs. Mulligan were talking about their children over a cup of tea.

"My daughter," said Mrs. O'Rourke, "is going to be a great actress some day. She's studying the dramatic arts. Only yesterday her teacher told me that all she needs is a course in electrocution to finish her off!"

"My son'll never be a great actor," said Mrs. Mulligan, "but he's a bright boy. D'ya know, he used to snore so loud he woke himself up? He has no trouble now. He sleeps in another room!"

*   *   *

SHEBANG

Monahan stumbled into a saloon, half-crocked. "Say," he said to the bartender, "how tall is a penguin?"

"About two and a half feet!"

"Thank God!" cried Monahan. "I thought I ran over a nun!"

* * *

Comedian Jackie Gleason is said to have stepped up to a Miami Beach bar and asked for a martini consisting of twenty-four parts gin and one part vermouth.

"Coming up!" said the bewildered bartender. "Like a slice of lemon peel twisted in it?"

"Look, buddy," snapped Gleason, "if I want a lemonade, I'll ask for it!"

"Every time I see you," screamed Mc-Closky's wife, "you've got a bottle in your pocket!"

"You don't expect me to keep it in me mouth all the time, do you?" replied her husband.

IRISH LOVE SONG
I'll Take You Home Again Kathleen,
'Cause The Martinis Have Turned You
Green.

*   *   *

Jack Luffee, genial host of Don Drysdale's Dugout, tells about the Irishman who knocked on Mrs. Connally's door.

"I'm sorry to have to tell you this, M'am," he said, "but your husband drowned in a vat of beer down at the brewery!"

"Oh, the poor man," exclaimed Mrs. Connally, "he didn't stand a chance!"

"Yes, he did! He got out twice to take a piss!"

*   *   *

McGuire marched up Fifth Avenue in the St. Patrick's Day parade. He forgot to make a left turn and wound up in the East River. It was the only water he touched all day.

*   *   *

KILLARNEY COCKTAIL
Two sips and you turn green!

*   *   *

Old Mrs. McIntyre came back from a Carribbean cruise with more than her five-

bottle liquor allotment. She thought she'd hide it from customs by pouring two fifths of gin into a large jar.

When the ship docked, the customs inspector looked at the jar suspiciously and asked, "What do you have in there?"

"Oh," said Mrs. McIntyre, "that's holy water."

The inspector opened the jar, tasted the contents and exclaimed, "Holy water, nothing! That's gin!"

"Glory be!" cried Mrs. McIntyre, "another miracle!"

* * *

McGinty was steering for a saloon when a Protestant minister stopped him. "My man, don't go into that saloon! Don't you know that the devil is with you?"

"I didn't recognize you, your Reverence," said McGinty, "but devil or not, come on anyhow—I'm settin' up the pair of us."

* * *

John: Poor Calhoun's sufferin' from that old Irish disease called Alcoholic Rheumatism.
Jack: What in the saints' name is Alcoholic Rheumatism?
John: He gets stiff in all the joints! Ha! Ha! Ha!

Bob Sherman, the California trailer sales king, tells this one at the showroom:

Donahue and Foyle stumbled out of a saloon, sat down on the sidewalk and looked up at the sky. "Ain't that a beautiful moon?" asked Donahue.

"G'wan," babbled Foyle, "that's the sun!"

"You're crazy! It's the moon!"

"Oh, no, it's the sun!"

At that moment, half-crocked Holligan came wobbling up the street. "Say, mister," cried Donahue, "is that the sun or the moon?"

"How should I know," answered Holligan, "I don't live around here!"

*   *   *

Handsome Bob Chenault, the actor, producer, and pride of the Hollywood Hackers golf fraternity, sent along this dilly:

How can you tell when an Irish patient is recovering?

When he tries to blow the foam off his medicine!

*   *   *

McArdle was married to an old shrew who nagged him all the time. In desperation, he began drinking and every night came home smashed. Hoping to cure him, his wife asked her neighbor Mrs. Steen for advice.

44

"The thing to do," suggested Mrs. Steen, "is to scare him to death. When he comes home at night, he takes a short cut through the cemetery. Scare the bejesus out of him, and he'll never drink again."

So Mrs. McArdle rented a devil's costume and hid behind a tombstone in the cemetery. That night, as McArdle stumbled by, she jumped out and growled, "Ahh, ah, ah!"

"Who are you?" slobbered McArdle.

"I am the devil!"

"Shake hands, I'm married to your sister!"

* * *

Hallihan and Flannigan were having a few at a new tavern in town. After an hour of heavy imbibing, Hallihan asked the bartender for the washroom. "Go to the door, left of the elevator," said the barkeep, "then walk down two steps and there you are."

Hallihan forgot to turn left. He opened the elevator door, took *one* step and fell down the shaft.

Ten minutes later, Flannigan followed Hallihan and saw him lying at the bottom of the shaft.

"Look out for that *second* step," shouted up Hallihan. "It's a son of a bitch!"

45

Mullanigan and Shayne were taking a little stroll. "At my funeral," said Mullanigan, "I want you to pour a bottle of Irish whiskey over me grave."

"I'll be glad to," said Shayne. "But would you mind if it passes through me kidneys first?"

IRISH DRUNK

An Irishman lying facedown in the gutter, looking down at his fellow man.

*　　*　　*

St. Patrick's is the holiday on which the Irish march up Fifth Avenue and stagger down Sixth Avenue.

*　　*　　*

"Me mother-in-law's gone to her final reward," and Donnegan to the barkeep in Tamney's Tavern, "and it's a twenty spot I'm needin' for a wreath. Could you be advancin' me the twenty?"

The bartender emptied his pockets and the cash register, but the total came to only $18.30.

"That'll do," said Donnegan quickly "I'll take the $1.70 in drinks!"

*　　*　　*

Father Callahan was at a pitch of fervor in his sermon on drinking. "What could be worse than drink?" he boomed.

"Thirst!" shouted Gannaway from the rear.

*　　*　　*

TOOHEY'S TOAST

At last I've found the perfect girl—
I could not ask for more.
She's deaf and dumb and oversexed
And she owns a liquor store.

48

GAELIC LEGEND

The tender young love of a beautiful girl
And the love of a strong young man
And the love of a mother for her child
Have gone on since time began.
But the greatest love, the love of love,
Even greater than that of a mother,
Is the all consuming, infinite love
Of one Irish drunk for another.

*   *   *

"Did you see how O'Flynn came to work today?"

"No."

"He was so loaded they made him use the freight elevator!"

*   *   *

McGonigle was staggering up the street from telephone pole to lamp post and back again. Father Daley stopped him and said, "Drunk again!"

"Are you?" said McGonigle. "So'm I, Father!"

"This is no time for levity!" admonished the priest. "After taking the pledge and promising me two weeks ago you'd never drink again! It's a sin against God and the Church and I'm sorry to be saying so!"

"You're sorry to see me so?"

"Indeed, I am!"

"Are you sure you're sorry?"

"Yes, very, very sorry!"

"Then if you're sorry," said McGonigle, "I'll forgive you, Father!"

"What's that pet name you have for Rafferty down at the saloon?"

"We call him Capistrano 'cause he's always ready for a few swallows."

* * *

"The doctor warned me against drinking," said Finley to his pal.

"Did he now?"

"Yes," said Finley. "He told me I'd have to limit me drinking to one a day. Right now I'm up to February 6, 1998!"

* * *

Branihan was driving down the road. By the way the car weaved in and out of traffic, you could tell that Branihan was pickled to the gills.

"Where d'ya think you're going?" asked the motorcycle cop who finally stopped him.

"I'm comin' home—hic—from a New Year's Eve party!"

"Are you kidding?" asked the cop. "New Year's was three weeks ago!"

"I know," said Branihan. "Thash why I figured I better be gettin' home."

* * *

O'Loughlin, visiting friends in Detroit, had returned to his hotel after a night of celebrating. He wobbled up to the desk clerk

and said: "Hey there, would'ja be givin' me the key to Room 712?"

Five minutes later, O'Loughlin lurched up to the desk again. "Give me the key to Room 712!"

"Hey, what's going on?" asked the clerk. "I just gave the key to Room 712 to some guy!"

"That was me! I fell out of the window!"

* * *

The owner of a saloon was awakened at four A.M. by a phone call from Monnelly. "When does your saloon open in the mornin'?" Monnelly asked.

"Sorry, you can't get in till noon."

"I don't want to get in—I want to get out!"

* * *

When aged Fennessy collapsed on the street, a crowd soon gathered and began making suggestions as to how the old fellow should be revived.

Maggie O'Reilly yelled: "Give the poor man some whiskey!"

No one paid any attention to her, and the crowd continued shouting out suggestions. Finally Fennessy opened one eye, pulled himself up on an elbow, and said weakly, "Will the lot o' ye hold yer tongues and let Maggie O'Reilly speak!"

Overheard at Scully's Saloon:
"I always go to Lafferty's birthday parties and help him drink up his presents."

"I'll never forget the day O'Shea dropped a bottle of Scotch on the floor. He's still got splinters in his tongue!"

"I woke up New Year's Day and I was really in the pink. So were the two elepants on the dresser."

"Brennan doesn't really drink. He just gargles with whiskey and sometimes it slips."

"Monahan's a very light sleeper. He wakes up at the crack of ice."

"McCoy works down at the docks. He once held up a ship launching for three hours. He wouldn't let go of the bottle."

Dennehy emigrated to New York and spent his first few days just wandering about the city. One afternoon he walked into a saloon and saw a sign behind the bar that read: *All the Beer You Can Drink for $1.*

"Okay, bartender," said Dennehy. "Gimme two dollars' worth!"

* * *

Gilfoyle stopped in at his favorite tavern on New York's Third Avenue. "Hey Mulkeen," he said to the bartender, "since when did you start puttin' sawdust on the floor?"

"That ain't sawdust, me bucko!" replied Mulkeen. "It's last night's furniture!"

* * *

Bracken and Nugent shuffled into an establishment for the thirsty and leaned on the bar. Bracken ordered a triple whiskey, swallowed it in one gulp, then swirled around and fell face-down onto the sawdust floor.

"That's what I like about Bracken," said the bartender to Nugent. "He always knows when he's had enough."

* * *

IRISH LULLABY
Empty the beer barrel slowly, Mother,
Father's been missing for days.

Culhane, obviously under the influence of heavy spirits, noticed a man coming out of a supermarket carrying two big bags of groceries.

"Look at him, spending all that money for food," said Culhane to no one in particular. "And I bet he ain't got a drop of liquor in the house!"

*   *   *

The train for New York had just pulled out of Washington. The passengers were all settling back in their seats comfortably when a tall, dignified gentleman entered the club car.

"I beg your pardon," he queried, "is there by chance an Irishman here?"

"I'm Irish," shouted Kilgallen, standing up proudly.

"Oh, that's wonderful!" boomed the man. "Could I be borrowin' your corkscrew?"

*   *   *

Ginty and Bannon reeled out of a London pub and climbed on a double-decker bus. Ginty insisted on going up topside. After a short time upstairs, he came lurching down to his pal, white as a sheet.

"What's wrong?" asked Bannon.

"Don't go upstairs!" sputtered Ginty. "There's no driver!"

Phelan, slightly under the weather, got on the Dublin-to-Cork bus. "Say," he said to the driver, "how far is it to Cork?"

"Seventy-six miles," replied the driver.

"Then how far is it from Cork to Dublin?"

"It's seventy-six miles. The same distance as it is from Dublin to Cork!"

"Not necessarily!" said Phelan. "It's only a week from Christmas to New Year's. But it's a helluva long time from New Year's to Christmas!"

*   *   *

"Prisoner, why did you knock down, beat up, and kick this man so shamefully?"

"I'm very sorry for that, your Honor! 'Twas all a mistake. I was a little under the weather and I thought it was me wife!"

*   *   *

TIPPERARY TOAST

Here's to the Frenchman *that loves his wine*
And the German *who loves his beer*
The Englishman *loves his 'alf and 'alf*
Because it brings good cheer.
The Scotchman *loves his whiskey straight*
Because it gives him dizziness.
But the Irishman *has no choice at all—*
So he drinks the whole damn business.

"Didja hear the news?" asked Reardon of his pal at the saloon. "Harrigan drank so much, his wife left him!"

"Waiter! Give me six boilermakers!"

* * *

"I notice Hogarty doesn't wear glasses any longer!"

"It's true! He read so much about the evils of drinking that he gave up reading!"

* * *

Comedian Jackie Gayle, one of Las Vegas' favorite funnymen, tells about Caddigan carrying a bottle of J&B in his hip pocket while marching in the St. Paddy's Day Parade.

He staggered down one of the side streets and was immediately hit by a truck. As he lay on the ground, Caddigan felt the wetness in his pants, and looked up at the sky. "Oh, Father in heaven," he cried, "please let it be blood!"

* * *

"Gilligan does other things beside drink!"

"What?"

"He hiccups!"

* * *

Boozed-up Bailey bobbed up to a man on the street, bummed a nickel from him, and walked over to a mail box. Opening it, he

dropped the nickel in the slot and then looked up at the clock on a nearby building.

"I'll be damned!" slobbered Bailey. "I've lost ten pounds and I just weighed myself last night!"

* * *

It happened on a midnight clear
Decidedly tight and breathing beer
Finn staggered to his wifie dear
And leaning toward her sleeping ear
He shouted loudly, without fear,
"NUTS TO YOU!"

* * *

"Why do you drink?" asked Hogan.

"Booze killed me mother," answered Kehoe, "and booze killed me father. I'm drinkin' for revenge!"

* * *

A preacher walked into a saloon and ordered a whiskey. The bartender put the glass on the bar. "I'm going to show you the evils of drink!" said the preacher. Whereupon he pulled a worm out of his pocket and dropped it in the glass. In a few seconds, the worm was dead.

"There," said the preacher to Sheehan who was draped over the bar. "Has that taught you a lesson?"

"Yeah," said Sheehan. "If you have worms, drink whiskey!"

McCall and O'Neil stumbled out of a saloon and decided to take the shortcut home. They began walking along the railroad tracks.

"These are the longest stairs I ever walked down," complained McCall.

"Yeah," agreed O'Neil, "and the banisters are so low!"

"Me brother Shamus just fell down the stairs with two pints of gin and didn't spill a drop!"

"How's that possible?"

"He kept his mouth closed!"

* * *

"Does your husband enjoy a bit of liquid refreshment?"

"Darlin, me old man's got the only bonded ulcers in Kilkenny."

* * *

Lanahan's hair kept falling out and he complained to his barber. "That stuff you gave me," he cried, "is terrible. You said two bottles of it would make me hair grow, but nothing's happened."

"I don't understand it," said the barber. "That's the best hair restorer made."

"Well," said Lanahan "I don't mind drinking another bottle, but it better work."

* * *

McInnerny celebrated New Year's Eve so well he woke up the next day in the hospital. His friend Shanley came to visit him.

"What happened last night?" asked McInnerny.

"You had quite a load on," answered Shanley. "You walked over to the window, climbed out on the sill, and announced you

were going to fly all over the borough of Manhattan!"

"My God, man," shouted McInnerny, "why didn't you stop me?"

"Tell you the truth," replied Shanley, "last night, I really thought you could do it!"

* * *

"Drinking doesn't affect me at all," bragged Bourke. "Last night, I was tippling the entire evenin' and I was in great shape. The only trouble was that people kept steppin' on me fingers!"

* * *

"Didn't you tell me, that O'Higgins joined Alcoholics Anonymous?"

"I did!"

"Then, what happened?"

"He never went to the meetin's. He used to drink and then send in the bottles."

* * *

A woman walking down the street was carrying a rabbit in a paper bag. Suddenly, she tripped, fell down, the bag broke, and the hare scooted away.

Kincaid, who had just come out of a saloon and saw the whole thing, staggered up to the woman and said, "Don't cry lady! It would've been an imbecile anyway—look at the ears!"

"I had a dream the other night," said Casey to his pal McGinn, "and it taught me a great lesson."

"What was it? asked McGinn.

"I dreamed I was in Rome and I had an audience with the Pope. 'Would I have a drink,' he asked me. Thinks I, 'Would a duck swim?' And seein' the whiskey and lemons and sugar on the sideboard, I told him I wouldn't mind a drop of punch. 'Cold or hot?' he asked me. 'Hot, your Holiness,' said I. An' that's where I made me mistake!"

"I don't see anything wrong—"

"His Holiness stepped toward the kitchen to boil the water and before he got back, I woke up!"

"What lesson did you learn?" asked McGinn.

"Next time," swore Casey, "I'll say, 'I'll take it cold, your Holiness, while the water's gettin' hot!' "

* * *

TOOLEY'S TOAST
Here's to our bartender—
may he never be low in spirits.

* * *

O'Hooley, just a broth of a lad, leaned against the bar and began a tirade against the bartender.

"What d'ya mean, I've had too much to drink!" shouted O'Hooley.

"Go on with you now," said the bartender. "I'll not be servin' you any more today!"

"I'll have everyone here know," he slobbered to all who could hear, "I'm the featherweight champion of the entire state of New Jersey."

"Be you now?" said the barkeep. "Well, one more peep out of you, me lad, and out you go—feathers and all!"

* * *

Silver-haired, golden-voiced tenor Patrick Sullivan tells about McAdoo getting blotto at the Branan wake. After an hour he tiptoed up to the hostess and said, "Do lemons have legs?"

"Lemons with legs?" exclaimed Mrs. Branan. "You must be losin' your mind!"

"In that case," said McAdoo, "I'm afraid I've just squeezed your canary into me whiskey!"

* * *

Mrs. Daley   (to drunk husband): Come on, darlin' let's be goin' to bed!

Mr. Daley: Might as well. I'll catch hell when I get home anyway.

"Would you say that O'Hagan drinks quite a bit?"

"I'm not sure. He says he drinks just to steady himself!"

"Yeah? Well, last night he got so steady he couldn't move!"

* * *

McCraken saw an ad in the papers for a man who didn't drink, could drive a car, and was reliable. The next day he showed up at the prospective employer's house.

"Do you drive a car?" asked the man.

"No!" said McCracken.

"Do you drink?"

"Yes!"

"If you can't drive and you drink, why did you answer the ad?"

"I just wanted to tell you," said McCracken, "that I'm not reliable!"

* * *

Dennahy and Finnegan had been at a bar, putting away brews for over two hours. "I have to go!" said Dennahy, motioning toward the men's room.

"Go ahead!" said Finnegan.

Five minutes later, Dennahy returned. "Did you go for me? asked Finnegan.

"No!" answered his friend, and headed back to the washroom.

When he returned, Dennahy said. "Aw, you didn't have to go!"

Flaherty sneaked into the bedroom and started making love to his sleeping wife, until she awakened and shouted, "Is that you?"

"It better be!" snorted Flaherty.

"When're you gonna stop this sinnin'?" she demanded. "Moody quit smokin'. Payne stopped his gamblin'. What're you gonna give up?"

"All right," said Flaherty through bloodshot eyes. "From now on, you sleep in the bedroom and I'll sleep in the spare room."

Three weeks went by, with Mrs. Flaherty sleeping alone. Finally, unable to contain herself for one more night, she tiptoed to the spare room and tapped lightly on the door. "What is it?" shouted Flaherty.

"I just wanted to tell ya," said his wife, "that Moody is smokin' again!"

* * *

Bill Jones, the posh Beverly Hills caterer, made this contribution:

Father Murray was waxing eloquent over the evils of liquor. "If I were to lead a donkey to a pail of water and a pail of beer," he exclaimed, "which would he drink?"

"The water!" grunted O'Morrison from the rear.

"Certainly," smiled the padre. "And why?"

"Because he's an ass!" said O'Morrison.

Highly inebriated, Clusky was tottering down the street when he bumped into the parish priest. "Have you been drinking, Clusky?" he asked.

"Oh, no! Just a little three fathers, feather!"

*   *   *

Doolan, in a decidedly tipsy state, boarded a bus and sat down in front of a minister reading the evening paper.

"I ain't goin' to heaven," bawled Doolan. "I ain't—*hic*—goin' to heaven!"

The minister continued to read his paper.

"I ain't goin' to heaven 'cause there ain't no heaven!"

"Well, go to hell then," said the preacher. "But be quiet about it!"

*   *   *

Hugh Wedlock, Jr., the great Irish comedy writer breaks up buddies with this bit of buffoonery:

For a holiday, Muleavy decided to go to Switzerland to fulfill a lifelong dream and climb the Matterhorn. He hired a guide and just as they neared the top, the men were caught in a snow slide.

Three hours later, a Saint Bernard

plowed through to them, a keg of brandy tied under his chin. "Hooray!" shouted the guide. "Here comes man's best friend!"

"Yeah," said Muleavy. "An' look at the size of the dog that's bringin' it!"

*   *   *

SHENANIGANS

How can you tell if an Irishman has class?
The words in his tattoo are spelled right.

* * *

Did you hear about the two Irish queers?
Patrick Fitzwillian and William Fitz-patrick.

* * *

IRISH WOMEN'S LIB
Erin Go Braless

* * *

FOR SALE
Second-hand tombstone.
Good buy for person named O'Hara.

Mrs. Carey had reached the grand age of 104. She was the oldest living being in County Cork. The newspaper sent a reporter to interview the old woman on her longevity.

"Have you ever been bedridden?" asked the newsman.

"Oh, many times," replied Mrs. Carey. "An' once in a sleigh, too!"

"Did you hear the news of the big explosion?"

"What explosion?"

"The explosion down at the brewery. 'Twas a terrible thing. Killed thirty-eight Englishmen and one Irishman!"

"Tch. Tch. The poor man!"

* * *

McMaken returned from a visit to his family in Galway. "What kind of a state is Ireland in today? asked his neighbor.

"Status quo!" replied McMaken. "In the south of Ireland we have the Catholics and in the north the Protestants, and they're at each other's throats as usual all the time. If only they were heathen so they could live together like good Christians!"

* * *

"I haven't been feelin' meself-lately!"

" 'Tis a good thing—that was a nasty habit you had!"

* * *

There once was a lass named McGoffin
Who was diddled amazingly often.
   At sex never bested
   She never was rested
Until she was screwed in her coffin.

Mahoney pleaded guilty, throwing himself on the mercy of the court. The judge nevertheless ordered a trial,, and to his amazement, the jury found Mahoney not guilty.

"What do you mean?" exclaimed the judge defiantly. "The man has confessed his guilt."

"Yes, your honor," agreed the foreman. "but you don't know Mahoney like we do. He's the most notorious liar in all County Cork and no twelve men who know his character can believe a word he's saying!"

* * *

Miss McKern walked up to the information desk in a hospital and asked to see the "*up*tern."

"I think you mean the *in*tern, don't you?" asked the nurse on duty.

"Yes, I guess I do," said the girl. "I want to have a contamination!"

"You mean *ex*amination," corrected the nurse.

"Well, anyway, I want to go to the fraternity ward."

"I'm sure," said the nurse, "that you're thinking of the *ma*ternity ward!"

"Uptern, intern; contamination, examination; fraternity, maternity . . . what's the difference?" shouted Miss McKern. "All I know is I haven't demonstrated in two months and I think I'm stagnant!"

Kelly Gilmore, the television commercials food expert, tells about Delaney migrating from Donegal to Denver. In the Colorado capital, he promptly registered at an unemployment agency.

"I guess it's pretty rough over there in Ireland these days," said the personnel director.

"Not too bad!" replied Delaney.

"What was the last job you had?"

"Tail gunner on a milk truck!"

* * *

Cuneen was taking his first plane ride, flying over the Rocky Mountains. The stewardess handed him a piece of chewing gum. "It's to keep your ears from popping at high altitudes," she explained.

When the plane landed, Cuneen rushed up to her. "Miss," he said, "I'm meetin' me wife right away. How do I get the gum out of me ears?"

* * *

"I tell you I won't have this room," protested Mrs. O'Dowd to the bellboy. "I'm not goin' to pay me good money for a closet with a measly little foldin' bed in it. If you think that just because I'm from the country—"

"Get in, lady, get in," interrupted the boy. "This isn't your room. This is the elevator!"

During World War II a company of soldiers from the Irish Army landed in North Africa and were being briefed by Sergeant Geehan. He was giving them tips on how to get along with the natives.

"Our job is to make friends with the natives," said Geehan to the men. "So, whatever you do, don't get into any arguments with them. If they say Africa is bigger than Ireland—agree with them."

* * *

A medical officer was testing the water supply. "What precautions do you take against infection?" he asked McGonigle, the sergeant in charge.

"We boil it first, sir," replied the NCO.

"Good."

"Then we filter it!"

"Excellent!"

"And then," said McGonigle, "just for safety's sake, we drink beer!"

* * *

O'Myer met Lohan, an old friend. "My gracious," said O'Myer, "I haven't seen you in thirty years, since we left Galway. How have you been?"

"I'm just fine!"

"You married?"

"Oh, yes!" said Lohan. "Me wife's an angel!"

"You're lucky," said O'Myer. "Mine's still alive!"

75

Corbett (to his wife) :Darlin', we haven't
made love in such a long time, tonight I'm goin' ta screw the bejabbers outa ya.

Wife: Over my dead body!

Corbett: An' why should tonight be any
different than any other night?

* * *

A man and a little boy entered a barber-
shop together. After the man received the
full treatment—shave, shampoo, manicure,
haircut, etc.—he placed the boy in the
chair. "I'm goin' to buy a green tie to wear
for the parade," he said. "I'll be back in a
few minutes."

When the boy's haircut was completed
and the man still hadn't returned, the
barber said, "Looks like your daddy's for-
gotten all about you."

"That wasn't my daddy," said the boy.
"He just walked up, took me by the hand,
and said, 'Come on, son, we're gonna get
a free haircut!' "

* * *

Rattigan was in court on the witness
stand. "What do you do for a living?"
boomed the caustic prosecuting attorney.

"I'm a sewer-digger," replied Rattigan.

"What do you think your social standing
is as a sewer-digger?" sneered the prose-
cutor.

"Well," said the witness, "I feel I'm

76

doin' a darn sight better than me father before me."

"What was he?" asked the attorney.

"A shyster lawyer!" said Rattigan.

*   *   *

Kilbane was standing in front of Tehan's Tavern when he saw a driverless car rolling slowly down the street. He ran to the car, jumped in, and pulled on the emergency brake with a jerk.

Kilbane got out and very proudly said to the man approaching him, "I stopped it!"

"I know, you jackass!" said the owner of the car. "I was pushing it!"

*   *   *

Hollywood producer Chuck Stuart tells about Mulvenny, who sold pencils in front of the courthouse. Attorney Caulfield stopped, gave him a dime as he had done for twenty years, but didn't take a pencil.

"Say, Counselor," snapped Mulvenny, as the lawyer started to walk away, "you've been doin' that now for years. You give me the money but you never take a pencil. How come?"

"I gave you that first dime twenty years ago," explained the barrister. "It brought me good luck. I'm successful, so I've been doing it ever since. Why do you ask?"

"Well," said Mulvenny, "startin' tomorra, pencils are a quarter!"

Did you hear about the two Irishmen who decided to drive from New York to Chicago?

They were afraid of the gas shortage—so they took two cars!

* * *

Tom McHugh, National Golf Courses promoter, saves this one to tell friends on March 17th:

A man lay in the middle of the street flat on his stomach, wriggling and writhing. Mrs. Gallivan pushed her way through the crowd gathered round him. "Why doesn't someone help this poor man?" she exclaimed.

Getting no reply from the crowd, Mrs. Gallivan jumped astride the man's back, stated she had just finished a course in first aid, and began to administer artificial respiration.

"I don't know what you're tryin' to do, lady," he grumbled, "but I'm tryin' to fix a wire down this manhole!"

* * *

The funeral service was over and Desmond, the undertaker, found himself standing beside an elderly gent. "One of the relatives?" asked the mortician.

"Yes, I am!" answered the senior citizen.

"How old are ya?"

"Ninety-four!"

"Hmmm," said Desmond, "hardly pays you to make the trip home!"

Michael and Agatha stood at the railing of the ship that was bringing them to New York City. As their vessel steamed up the Hudson River, the young colleen noticed ferry boats plying back and forth.

"They've got a front at both ends!" exclaimed Agatha to her husband. "Why is that?"

" 'Tis quite simple, me love," said Michael. "Sure'n it's so they can go both ways at the same time!"

* * *

This editorial supposedly appeared in a Tralee newspaper:

"The recent census shows that most Irishmen marry late in life. The ideal will be reached when all women are married and all men are single."

* * *

What do they call a bunch of people watching a neighbor beat up his wife?

An Irish theater party!

* * *

Nolan was complaining to a friend that his neighbor, McGraw, didn't participate in the election.

"McGraw never voted," said Nolan. "He wouldn't know how to vote. McGraw doesn't even pull the curtain when he takes a shower."

Actress Jeanine Riley, the beautiful television and motion picture actress, tells about McCormick the sea captain.

It seems Captain McCormick became confused one day on the bridge and almost rammed the admiral's flagship. Signal flags broke out from the admiral's vessel.

"It's for you, sir!" said an ensign to the befuddled captain. "It says, 'You *blank blank* landlubber, what the *blank* do you think you're doing with that *blank blank* tub of yours?'"

"Quick now, lad!" ordered the captain. "Better take that down to the signal room and have it decoded!"

* * *

A farmer from Cork named O'Doole
Has a long and incredible tool.
He can use it to plow
Or to diddle a cow
Or just as a cue-stick at pool.

* * *

Hugh Stevenson, chief aide to Los Angeles City Councilman Joel Wachs, came up with this doozy:

During the recent Irish elections a candidate was pleading his cause. "All we ask," he shouted from the platform, "is another two years to complete our program!"

"And what, me boy," demanded a voice from the back, "*is* your program?"

"To stay in for another two years!" answered the candidate.

*   *   *

O'Morrison and Duffy were friendly enemies. Both were saloon keepers. And they never missed a chance to put something over on one another.

O'Morrison decided to run for Alderman and tried to get Duffy to vote for him. "I wouldn't vote for you," said Duffy, "if you were St. Peter himself!"

"If I were St. Peter," countered O'Morrison, "you wouldn't be in my ward."

*   *   *

SKIBBEREEN FOLK SONG
Everybody Calls Bridget Spry Because She's Fat in the Can.

*   *   *

A young Irish tenor, anxious to make it big in show business, kept pestering a theatrical agent for work. "Kid," said the agent, "I want to book you when the time is right—not before!"

"When is that?"

"When I get an offer for you!"

John F. Kennedy had many admirable character traits, but none more desirable than his keen sense of humor. He loved making an audience laugh. Here are some samples of his great Irish wit:

Accused of financing the 1960 presidential campaign with his father's millions, Mr. Kennedy joked about the false accusation like this:

"I just received the following telegram from my generous father: DEAR JACK: DON'T BUY A SINGLE VOTE MORE THAN IS NECESSARY. I'LL BE DAMNED IF I'M GOING TO PAY FOR A LANDSLIDE."

JFK addressing an expensive fund-raising dinner in his honor: "I am deeply touched, but not as deeply touched as you have been by coming to this dinner."

When chastised for making his own brother, Robert F. Kennedy, the attorney general, the President answered: "I don't think there's anything wrong in the kid getting some experience before going into private practice."

The late James J. Walker, once mayor of New York City, was a brash but lovable Irishman. His administration had been scandal-ridden and he himself accused of taking graft. His answer? "I never took more than I needed."

The most famous tale told about Jimmy Walker was about the time His Honor was ill in the hospital and for some medical reason had to be fed rectally through a tube. After three or four days he began to feel better and noticed that the nurse was an extremely cute Irish girl. One afternoon, when she had finished feeding him, the Mayor said, "Look, tomorrow, bring another tube and we'll have lunch together!"

* * *

McNellis ran for Congressman. But he was so unpopular, one year he ran unopposed and still lost.

* * *

"When the enemy gets within a hundred yards of us," declared Corporal Callahan to his men, "I want you all to retreat. Bein' a bit lame, I'm startin' now!"

"The Irish are the best fighters in the world!" announced Connors' fellow workers on a lunch break. "They can lick anybody in the world!"

"Oh, they not be such good fighters!" said Swenson the Swede. "My brothers, Ole, Nels, Sven, and two other fellows, we licked one of them yesterday."

Charlene Reveal, proprietor of the fashionable Westwood, California, women's boutique, regales customers with this nugget:

"How could you let him get away?" the desk sergeant screamed at McNutt, the rookie cop. "Did you watch all the exits like I told you?"

"Yes, sir," replied McNutt. "But he must've left by one of the entrances!"

*   *   *

Tim: Why do you always show your stupidity?

Tom: What's the use of having something if you can't show it?

*   *   *

O'Hare and McGinn worked in a large machine shop. O'Hare was oiling a huge fly wheel, almost twenty-five feet wide. Someone called his name, and when O'Hare looked away, his sleeve got caught in the wheel and he was whirled around and around and around.

McGinn was speechless. He stood frozen with horror. Suddenly, he jumped into action, pulled the switch and the machine slowly stopped.

McGinn picked O'Hare up in his arms and said, "Speak to me! Speak to me!"

"Why should I?" said O'Hare. "I passed you six times and you didn't speak to *me!*"

* * *

IRISH QUEER
Gaelic

* * *

Crime is on such a rise in the major cities, police have begun to organize into what they call the Buddy System. Here's an example:

"Collins! Let's go up that dark alley and see what's makin' all that noise!"

"Not me, buddy!"

* * *

Nellie bought a brand new dress
'Twas flimsy and quite thin,
She asked me how I liked it
And I answered with a grin
(Singing) WAIT TILL THE SUN SHINES, NELLIE

* * *

LONDONDERRY EROS
She Was Only an Irish Colleen but She Certainly Wasn't Green.

There may be a Shamrock Hotel in Ireland but the most famous one by that name is in Houston. One night a guest walked up to Corrigan, the desk clerk.

"Is this a respectable hotel?" asked the man.

"It is, sir!" answered Corrigan.

"Well," said the guest, "I was just on the fourth floor and I saw a naked man chasing a naked woman through the halls."

"Did he catch her?" asked the desk clerk.

"No." said the man.

"Then it's still a respectable hotel!" replied Corrigan.

A woman in a car stalled at the corner and the traffic light kept changing. Red ... yellow ... green ... red ... yellow ... green.

Finally, Officer McNally strolled over—it was downhill—and said, "Whatsa matter lady, ain't we got any colors you like?"

* * *

Hear about Feeney the fairy?
He'll grant you three wishes if you'll grant him one!

* * *

Tim: Just remember what it says in the Bible: "Don't worry—here comes the quilt!"
Tom: You idiot! That's "Fear Not—the comforter cometh!"

* * *

Frank O'Connor, Universal Pictures exec, reveals his Irish pride with this bit of persiflage:

The British missionary was trying to convince the Hindu to join Christianity: "Wouldn't you like to go to Heaven when you die?"

"Not me," said the Hindu. "If Heaven were any good, you British would have grabbed it years ago!"

90

A small town in Ireland has this poster with the legend:

Help Support Your Local Police!
Bribe Them.

* * *

"What makes you think the English even have a sense of humor?" asked Mc-Millin during an argument with Dunleavy.

"Ah, but the English do know humor!" said Dunleavy. "An Englishman laughs at a joke three times. Once when he hears it, once when it is explained to him, and once when he understands it."

* * *

"I thought I was drownin' for sure," said McSweeney. "I was goin' down for the third time, mind you, and suddenly me whole life passed before me eyes. In clear, sharp pictures—it all came back to me!"

"I don't suppose," said Ferguson, "one of those sharp, clear pictures was one of me lendin' you ten bucks back in the spring of 1948?"

* * *

PENDERGAST'S POLITICAL
PROMISE
If I should run for office
I wouldn't be a dope,
I'd only kiss the babies who
Are old enough to vote.

91

"Did you bring any money?" asked Mc-Nish of his pal on the way to the race track.

"No," said Griffith, "me wife blew it all on the rent!"

* * *

"Did you place a wager at the Sweepstakes?"

"I did. The horse I bet on was so sway-backed he had to walk on tiptoes to keep his stomach from draggin'."

* * *

Comedy writer-author Jack Douglas, dedicated one of his books:
To Barry and Ella Fitzgerald

* * *

"Is there any work in Ireland for a musician?"

"Things is so tough over there these days, MacNamara's Band is playin' Bar Mitzvohs."

* * *

There was a young fellow named
    Sweeney
Whose girl was a terrible meanie.
    The hatch of her snatch
    Had a catch that would latch;
She could only be screwed by Houdini.

"Isn't it grand that St. Patrick's Day comes before April 15!"

"Yeah, now we can at least wave the green before the government takes it away!"

* * *

IRISH LOTTERY COCKTAIL
One glass and bingo!

* * *

"At the parade today, did you notice how well Coogan beat the big bass drum?"

"Indeed, I did!"

"I found out why. He had a picture of his mother-in-law pasted on it!"

* * *

O'Higgins came from an inland Ireland town, and on his arrival in New York, reached the battery. For three days he hung around the pier where a great anchor lay on the planks.

"Is there anything I can do for you?" asked a stevedore who noticed him staring at the giant anchor.

"No, thank ye," replied O'Higgins. "I'm just waitin' ta see who the man is that can swing that pick!"

Dick Barth, Hollywood talent agent with Wm. Cunningham and Associates, regales golf cronies with this one:

Doheny and Garrett passed a butcher shop. On the window was printed: *Kosher Meat Market*.

"I've seen that sign many times," said Doheny. "What does it mean?"

"To you that sign means nothing and to me that sign means nothing," said Garrett. "But to the Jewish people—that's *Duncan Hines!*"

* * *

Hanseatic Cruise Director Tony Noice, as proud an Irish storyteller as ever sailed the Caribbean, provided this yarn from his collection:

Father Gannon went to visit Finn in the hospital. "I'm goin' to pray," said the priest, "that you'll forgive Kilroy for hitting you over the head with that bottle."

"Sure'n you might be wastin' yer time, Father," said Finn. "Why not wait till I get well and then pray for Kilroy!"

* * *

Cassidy and Cohen were on a ship and argued every day about the eternal life and where man went after death. Then one day, Cohen fell mortally ill and was buried at sea. As was the age-old custom, Cohen's body was weighed down with coal.

"I knew where he was goin' all the time," Cassidy commented, "but I never dreamed the heathen'd have to be takin' his own fuel!"

*　*　*

A famed vaudevillian used to sing this parody to "Where The River Shannon Flows":

Three Hebrews once were talkin'
Of the time when they would die,
And each was undecided as to
Where he would like to lie.
"Jerusalem," said Levi.
"New York," said Reubenstein.
But when it came to Ginsberg
He said, "The only place for mine

Is where the river Shannon's flowing,
It's there I would repose,
In an Irish cemetery
With some shamrocks 'neath my nose.
And the devil he'll be searching
For me, I suppose,
But he'll never think of looking for
*　　Ginsberg*
Where the river Shannon flows."

*　*　*

SAINTS

McKee: Have you christened your new baby yet?

Ahern: Indeed, we have.

McKee: An' what did you call it?

Ahern: Hazel.

McKee: With two hundred forty-seven saints to name the kid after, you had to go and name it after a nut!

* * *

"And how much of that stack of hay did you steal, Kavanaugh?" the priest asked at confession.

"I might just as well confess to the whole stack, your Reverence," said Kavanaugh. "I'm goin' after the rest of it tonight!"

Young Kerrigan sat in the confessional. "Forgive me, Father, for I have sinned," said the youth. "I've had intercourse with one of the women in this congregation."

"Who was it?" asked the priest.

"I couldn't betray her," said the boy.

"Was it, by any chance, the comely Mrs. Nolan?"

"No, sir!"

"Was it the lovely Mrs. Walsh, then?" The lad shook his head.

"Was it Garrett's good-looking daughter?"

Kerrigan refused to answer and left the church. Outside, he ran into one of his cronies. "Did Father Skelly give you absolution?"

"No," said Kerrigan, "but he did give me three good leads!"

*　　*　　*

"I hear you went to the ball game last Sunday instead of goin' to church."

"That's a lie! And I've got the fish to prove it!"

*　　*　　*

Dennis Patrick, known for his many fine roles in motion pictures and television, often treats fellow actors to his Irish wit. The following is a classic:

A Protestant minister was given a brand-new car by his congregation, and he was

98

driving it through downtown Dublin. Suddenly, the car in front of him came to a screeching stop and the minister crashed into it.

The furious clergyman climbed out and stormed up to the car in front of him with murder in his eyes. Then he noticed that the driver of the other vehicle was a Catholic priest.

"Your Reverence," said the minister through clenched teeth, "were it not for the fact that I am a man of the cloth, I would be tempted to thrash you to within an inch of your life!"

"Your Reverence," said the priest, sticking his head out the window, "were it not that I too am a man of the cloth, and that it happens to be a Friday, I would be tempted to bite your balls!"

* * *

A wealthy farmer went to church one Sunday. After services he said to the priest, "Father, that was a damned good sermon you gave, damned good!"

"I'm happy you liked it," said the priest. "But I wish you wouldn't use those terms in expressing yourself."

"I can't help it," said the rich farmer. "I still think it was a damned good sermon. In fact, I liked it so much I put a hundred-dollar bill in the collection basket."

"The hell you did!" replied the priest.

Ireland's antipathy toward England is legendary. Therefore, no collection of Irish humor would be complete without the following two stories:

Boyle sat in a Belfast confessional. "Bless me, Father, for I have sinned," he said. "I've blown up three hundred miles of English railroad!"

"All right, my son," admonished the priest. "For penance, do the stations!"

Young O'Donnell rushed into a church, placed his machine gun under a pew and entered the confessional. "Father," he said breathlessly, "I've just mowed down two British lieutenants!"

Hearing no response he went on: "I also knocked off a British captain!"

When there was still no response from the priest, O'Donnell said, "Father, have ye fainted?"

"Of course, I haven't fainted," replied the confessor. "I'm waitin' for you to stop talkin' politics and commence confessin' your sins!"

* * *

Mrs. McGiklin confessed to the priest that she had committed adultery. "Was it against your will?" asked her confessor.

"No," said Mrs. McGiklin. "It was against the cupboard, and heavens you should've heard the china rattle!"

* * *

Father Donovan ran into O'Keefe. "I haven't seen you all summer," greeted the priest. "In fact, I don't believe you've been to church since last May."

"Father, when it's hot, you can't expect people to sit in church," said O'Keefe. "Nowadays, everything is air-conditioned —movies, offices, restaurants. And churches should be, too. Otherwise, attendance'll drop!"

"There's one place that's been without air-conditioning for ages," said Father Donovan, "and I understand attendance is holding up well there!"

* * *

Father McElroy was paying a visit to the O'Sheel family who lived quite a ways out in the country. Suddenly, the young son came bursting into the house holding a rat by the tail.

"He's dead," said young O'Sheel to his mother. "We clobbered him and stamped on him till—"

At that moment he spotted Father Mc-Elroy and said, "Till God called him home!"

Sister Marie became a nun in a cloistered order. That's one where they're not allowed to talk. After five years, the Mother Superior sent for her. "You've done such excellent work the past five years, I'm going to allow you to speak one sentence.

"My mattress is lumpy," said Sister Marie.

"You'll just have to get by," said the Mother Superior. "We're very poor here!"

Five years later, Sister Marie was sent for again. "You've done so well these past five years," said the Mother Superior, "I'm going to let you speak two sentences!"

"My mattress is still lumpy," said Sister Marie. "And I'm cold!"

"We are a very poor order. You'll just have to do the best you can!"

Another five years passed and once again the nun stood before the woman in charge. "This time I'm going to allow you to speak three sentences!"

"My mattress is still lumpy," grumbled Sister Marie. "My room is still cold! And I quit!"

"It's just as well," said the Mother Superior. "You've done nothing but complain from the moment you got here!"

*   *   *

Madigan and O'Skelly were being sentenced for murder. "Do you have anything to say?" asked the judge.

"I'm sorry they caught us!" said Madigan.

102

"Then you confess, now, that you killed the man?"

"We might've done it," said O'Skelly, "if it don't do no harm to say so now.

"How did you do it?" the judge inquired.

"I struck him with a stone," answered Madigan. "And O'Skelley hit him with a shillelagh and then we buried him."

"What did you do before you buried him?"

"We searched him!" said O'Skelley.

"And what did you find?"

"Two dollars and a roast beef sandwich!" replied Madigan.

"You kept the money, I'm sure, but what did you do with the sandwich?"

"We was hungry," said O'Skelly, "so we ate the bread and threw away the meat."

"Why'd you throw away the roast beef?"

"Your honor," said Madigan, "it was on a Friday. It'd been a *sin* to eat the meat!"

* * *

McDonnell had just come out of the confessional and was walking up the aisle of the church saying his Rosary for penance.

A woman who had just finished praying had caught her dress in her heel in attempting to get up. "I beg your pardon, sir," she said to McDonnell, "would you please pick up my dress!"

"No m'am! For doing that, I'm doing this!"

An acrobatic dancer went to confession one morning. Evidently, she felt ecstatic afterward, for when she came out of the confessional she began doing backward flips and somersaults and spins.

Just then, two Irish ladies walked into the church. "Goodness gracious!" whispered one of them. "Look what Father Phelan is givin' for penance today and me without me drawers on!"

O'Nolan was selling tickets for a church benefit. "I'm sorry I can't buy one," said his friend Clancy. "I won't be able to attend, but my spirit'll be there with you."

"Good," said O'Nolan. "I have a two-dollar, a three-dollar, and a five-dollar ticket. Where would you like your *spirit* to sit?"

* * *

Just out of the seminary, Father McLaughlin was assigned to a parish in Chicago. Three weeks after he arrived, Father McLaughlin walked into the church and stopped dead in his tracks. Kneeling at the altar, praying, was Jesus Christ.

The young priest rushed into his superior's office. "Father Conlon," he exclaimed. "Come quick! Our Savior is in the church!"

The two men rushed back into the church and sure enough, there was Christ at the altar. "What should we do?" whispered Father McLaughlin.

"Look busy!" answered the older priest.

* * *

Bishop Fulton J. Sheen was scheduled for a television interview in a Hollywood studio which was also filming a children's fairy tale program. The prelate decided to get a cup of coffee.

Resplendent in his scarlet skull cap and

silk cape, his Eminence strolled into the studio cafeteria. The waitress, having served actors in costume all day, walked over to his table. "All right," she said, "what's yours, Robin Red Breast?"

* * *

When Milton Berle was Mr. Television on Tuesday nights, his reign as Number One Star was ended by Bishop Sheen. Berle met Sheen shortly after the Bishop had replaced him as Number One and graciously congratulated him. "I don't deserve all the credit," said His Eminence, smiling. "I just have better writers than you do!"

Berle laughed, and then the Bishop added: "But don't feel too badly, Milton. My writers are all nice Jewish boys—Matthew, Mark, Luke, and John."

* * *

Vaudevillian Eddie Parkes swears this is a true story:

During the vaudeville days, a Chicago theatrical agent provided all the performers for the Catholic charity benefits throughout the city.

The agent was in the confessional and said, "Father, I know you don't know who I am, but I have a long confession to make."

"It's all right, my son," said the priest. "Just get us a singer, a juggler, a comic, and a piano player for next Saturday night."

A Presbyterian minister arrived at Kennedy International Airport and hailed a tax driven by Heffernan, a staunch Catholic.

"Take me to Christ Church," said the clergyman.

Forty minutes later, they drove up Fifth Avenue and stopped in front of St. Patrick's Cathedral. "Is this Christ Church?" asked the minister.

"If he ain't in there," replied Heffernan, he ain't in town!"

* * *

At a recent Las Vegas appearance, Danny Thomas quoted San Francisco Mayor Joseph Alioto as telling them at a Boys Town of Italy Banquet:

Father Quigley was talking to one of his Irish parishioners. "I understand you're still working for that Italian construction firm," he said, "How many times have I told you, a Hibernian shouldn't work for Dagos. How is your boss treating you?"

"Just fine," answered the Irishman. "How's yours treatin' you?"

* * *

Sister Mary Elizabeth had been walking down a street when she was grabbed by a man, dragged into an alley, and raped.

"Oh, woe is me!" she cried, when the

rapist finished. "How will I ever tell Mother Superior I was raped twice."

"What do you mean, twice?" asked her attacker.

"You're going to do it again, aren't you?" sighed the nun.

* * *

Father Dillon had been summoned to give the last rites to a man hurt in a factory accident.

"Do you believe in God the Father, God the Son, and God the Holy Ghost?" asked the priest.

"Father, here I am dyin' and you're botherin' me with riddles!"

* * *

Father Moynihan had been sent as a Catholic missionary to a tribe of cannibals in Africa. In a short time, he had achieved great success. He convinced the cannibals that on Friday they should only eat fishermen.

* * *

Did you hear about the Irishman who walked down the street kicking children, pinching women, and breaking windows?

He was on his way to confession and didn't have enough material.

109

Writer Brendan Behan lay on his death bed in St. Anthony's Hospital. He beckoned the nun who had been caring for him and said, "Bless you, sister! May all your sons be Bishops!"

* * *

There was a horrible automobile crash and the driver of the car lay on the side of the road dying. A passerby said to him kindly, "Why don't you say a prayer?"

"I don't know any," said the stricken man.

"Haven't you had any contact with religion?"

"As a boy, we used to live next to a Catholic Church!"

"That's it!" said the well-wisher. "Just repeat what you heard in the church!"

"Okay," said the injured man. "Under the B—15! Under I—22!"

* * *

RHYTHM SYSTEM
Vatican Roulette

* * *

Jim Poulos, in Hanna, Wyoming, breaks up his bar customers with this lulu:
Before an important Notre Dame football game a priest entered the Irish locker

room to bless the players and remind them that it was a sin to use the Lord's name profanely.

After offering up a prayer for victory, the priest said, "Have any of you ever spoken the Lord's name in vain?"

No one moved. Then from the back of the room a player slowly raised his hand. "Tell me, son," asked the priest, "did you ever speak God's name wastefully?"

"Well, Father," said the fullback, "it was during our game with Michigan. The quarterback handed me the ball. I cut off tackle, bounced off their linebacker, side-stepped two other guys, ran to the side-lines, dodged a man, cut back to the op-posite side of the field, outran the rest of their team . . . I crossed the goal line, looked down, and said, 'Jesus Christ, where's the ball?' "

* * *

A crook held up a man and it turned out to be a priest. "You ought to be ashamed of yourself," said the Catholic clergyman, "especially on St. Patrick's Day."

"I'm sorry, Father," said the hoodlum, "please don't lecture me! I won't do it again!"

"All right, and here's a cigar for you!"

"No thanks, Father! I gave up smoking for Lent!"

111

Father Moran was delivering his Sunday Sermon. "Someday," he said, "every man in this parish will die!"

Suddenly, the priest heard McLean laughing in the third row. But he continued. "As I was, saying, every man in this parish will die!"

Again, McLean began chortling. Father Moran looked at him and said, "Why do you laugh when I say everyone in this parish will die some day!"

"Ha! Ha!" exclaimed McLean. "I'm not from this parish!"

Father Donnelly in his sermon was describing the horrors of sin. "Stand up," he shouted, "all ye who prefer sin!"

Keenan, who had been half dozing in the back row leaped to his feet. "Do *you* prefer sin?" roared the priest.

"I beg your pardon, Father," said Keenan, "I thought you said gin!"

* * *

McDowel stumbled out of a saloon right into the arms of Father Logan. "Inebriated again!" declared the priest. "Shame on you! When are you going to straighten out your life?"

"Father," asked McDowell. "What causes arthritis?"

"I'll tell you what causes it! Drinking cheap whiskey, gambling, and carousing around with loose women. How long have you had arthritis?"

"I don't," jawed McDowell. "The Bishop has it!"

* * *

Pat O'Brien, remembered for his superb movie portrayal of Knute Rockne, told this story on the Mike Douglas Show:

A Notre Dame linebacker went to confession. The priest was a bit absent-minded and had a habit of marking the number of sins on his sleeve with a piece of chalk in order to mete out the proper penance.

114

"Father," said the football star, "I ran clear across the field to clip a player."

"That was very wrong, my son," said the priest, making a mark.

"When he fell, I kicked him in the teeth!"

"That's terrible! Will you never learn Christianity?" (Four more chalk marks).

"And when the referee wasn't looking, I belted him in the jaw!"

"Saints preserve us! You're a disgrace to your fine coach and the college!" by this time, the chalk marks were clear up to the priest's elbow. "And what was the team you were playin', my son?

"Southern Methodist!" replied the player.

"Oh," said the priest, rubbing off every mark on his sleeve. "I guess boys will be boys!"

* * *

Pretty Miss Kinneen sat in the confessional. "Father," she said, "I want to confess that I let my boyfriend kiss me!"

"Is that all you did?" asked the priest.

"Well, no. I let him put his hand on my leg, too!"

"And then what?"

"And then I let him pull down my panties."

"And then?"

"Then he took out his thing and put it in me hand!"

115

"And then, and then?"

"And then me mother walked into the room!"

"Oh, shit!" sighed the priest.

* * *

Father Flaherty was lecturing his parishioners. "Don't smoke," he declared, "it has killed millions. Don't drink or overeat or carouse late at night. It has killed millions!"

"Tell me, Father," cried Coolahan from the rear of the church. "What kills the people who live right?"

* * *

Television and motion picture actor, Phil Proctor, tells about Mrs. Leary having a chat over tea with Father Driscoll.

"Do you get a chance to read much?" asked the matron.

"As a matter of fact," replied the priest, "I just finished *Everything You Always Wanted to Know about Sex But Were Afraid to Ask!*"

"Why, Father," exclaimed Mrs. Leary, "I'm shocked to think that you'd buy a book like that!"

"I didn't buy it!" retorted the man of the cloth. "A friend gave it to me as a wedding present!"

Sisters Margaret Alice and Francis Katherine were out walking along a side street. Suddenly, they were grabbed by two men, dragged into a dark alley, and raped.

"Father, forgive them," said Sister Margaret Alice, "for they know not what they do!"

"Shut up!" cried Sister Francis Katherine. "This one does!"

* * *

Maureen, an Irish lass, and Irving, a Jewish boy, fell in love. "If you want to marry my daughter," said the girl's father, "you'll have to become a Catholic!"

Irving agreed, and for the next six months he studied and learned everything he could about Catholicism. In fact, during this time, he never missed a Sunday in church.

Then one day, Maureen, with tears in her eyes, went to her father. "Irving," she stammered, "isn't going to marry me!"

"Why not?" asked her father. "He's developed a real interest in our religion."

"That's the trouble," explained the grief-stricken girl. "Irving likes Catholicism so much he's decided to become a priest!"

* * *

117

THE END . . .

of the Irish jokes, that is. Please turn the book over and start again, to read the Jewish jokes. (Unless you're Irish, of course, in which case you merely have to reread this stuff—but *without* promising yourself a beer for each joke you understand.)

NOTE

If you are Irish and find it difficult to laugh at yourself or if you have become angry, there is one way to have a laugh and lessen your anger. Follow these instructions carefully:

(1) Every time you see the word Irish (or any slang meaning same) substitute one of the following words:

Polish, Italian, Chinese, German, British, Icelandic, Brazilian, Canadian, Filipino, Hungarian, Egyptian, Russian, Australian, Norwegian, African, Korean, Gypsy, Afghanistanian, etc. See how easy it is to be funny!

(2) Now you can read the Jewish jokes . . . and by the way, we've already done a book on Polish and Italian jokes, in case you'd appreciate a laugh at *their* expense.

UP THE IRISH!